Indian Presidency
and
Successive Presidents

Indian Presidency and Successive Presidents

M.L. Ahuja

Foreword
Dr GVG Krishnamurty
Former Election Commissioner of india

SYNERGY
Synergy Books India
(A unit of Bookwell Publications)
New Delhi

First Edition 2013

ISBN: 978-93-82059-10-3

Published by:
Synergy Books India
(A unit of Bookwell Publications)
24/4800 Ansari Road, Darya Ganj
New Delhi-110002
Phone: 011-23268786, 23257264
Fax: 011-23281315
Email: Synergybooksindia@gmail.com
bookwell@vsnl.net

Printed in India:
Glorious Printers, New Delhi.

Dr GVG Krishnamurty
(Doctor of Laws, Jhansi & London, Honoris Causa)
Former Election Commissioner of India

Foreword

Presidents or Rashtrapatis in India eminently symbolize the majesty, sovereignty, dignity and solidarity of Indian people. Therefore, the President is always held in high esteem as its first citizen, whom the nation trusts to be a friend, philosopher and guide to lead the country on the path of peace, progress and prosperity, as per the Constitution and the law. Further, whether it is parliamentary or presidential system of democracy, the President of a nation, whether elected directly or indirectly, is bound by the oath that he will uphold the Constitution and the unity and integrity of the country.

In regard to the extent, scope and role of the powers of President of India, there has been a debate, raised by Dr Rajendra Prasad while inaugurating the Indian Law Institute in 1960 whether or not the President has any active role to play during his tenure in the affairs of the country and whether the British analogy of the constitutional head in the parliamentary system applies at all and, if so, to what extent.

Dr Rajendra Prasad's observations remain valuable and relevant even today in examining and assessing the role the President should play in the coming decades.

> *The question which, I should like to be studied and investigated is the extent to which and of the matters in respect of which, if any, the powers and functions of President differ from those of the Sovereign of Great Britain. Further, it may also be considered if the procedure by which the President is elected and is liable to be removed or impeached introduces any difference, constitutionally speaking between the President and British monarch. Generally, what are the points in respect of which the powers and functions of the two are the same and what are the points, if any, and the extent to which they differ? ... how far, we are entitled to invoke and incorporate into our*

written Constitution by interpretation the conventions of the British Constitution which is an unwritten Constitution. This is necessary in view of the fact that our conditions and problems are not on par with the British and it may not be desirable to treat ourselves as strictly bound by the interpretations which have been given from time to time to the expressions in England.

A seven judge Bench of the Supreme Court in *Shamsher Singh*'s case (AIR 1974 S.C. 2192) observed:

The Assembly chose a slightly modified version of the British Cabinet System. India was to have a President, indirectly elected for a term of five years, who would be a Constitutional Head of State in the manner of the monarch in England ... As in England, there was to be a Council of Ministers headed by the Prime Minister and collectively responsible to Parliament to aid and advise the head of State. The President was to be the nominal head of the Executive, the Prime Minister the real head.

In spite of this interpretation by the Supreme Court, the debate has continued unabated till date, whether the President, as an elected Head of State by all elected members of Parliament and members of State Legislatures in the country, in contrast to the hereditary British monarch, is armed with any real powers to be exercised in the interest of the country to safeguard the unity and integrity, particularly in response to a national call to act in times of political upheavals and crises in the larger interest of the country.

The question to which we must find an answer is: "Should we blindly or slavishly follow British practices, conventions or interpretations in independent India even after 65 years of independence when they could be totally dispensed with in view of the entirely different political, economic and social conditions and aspirations of the post-independence generations of Indian people. And this too even after having developed exemplary constitutional jurisprudence as the largest practicing democracy among 120 democratic countries of the world.

Incidentally, the question of applicability of British conventions and practices in a free country (West Nigeria which was formerly under British) with a written Constitution came up before the Privy Council in England in 1967 in the case *Adegburo* vs *Akniktola* (1963, Law Reports, Appeal cases, England, p.614). The Privy Council was very explicit when they said while interpreting a written Constitution as follows:

> *The Constitution of West Nigeria is now contained in a written instrument in which it has been sought to formulate with precision the powers and duties of the various agencies that it holds in balance. That instrument now stands in its own right and, while it may well be useful on occasions to draw on British practice or doctrine. In interpreting a doubtful phrase whole origin can be traced or to study decisions on the Constitution itself that has to be interpreted and applied and his wording can never be over-ridden by the extraneous principles of other Constitutions which are not explicitly incorporated in the formulae that has been chosen as the frame of the Constitution.* (emphasis supplied).

As on today in the 21st century, when India has emerged as one of the powerful nations and as the largest practicing democracy, it is time to redefine the role of the President under the Constitution in the light of the spirit of a free and emerging India rather than depending on archaic British conventions and practices.

Article 74 and 75 of the Indian Constitution deal with the Council of Ministers. According to Article 74

> *There shall be a Council of Ministers with the Prime Minister at the head to aid and advice the President in the exercise of his functions.*

Under Article 75, the President is to exercise the power to appoint the Prime Minister and appointing other ministers is done by him on the advice of the Prime Minister. Secondly, the ministers would be holding the office during the pleasure of the President. Thirdly, the Council of Ministers would be collectively responsible to the House of People. Fourthly, before a minister enters upon his office, President has to administer to him the oath of office and of secrecy, according to the forms set out for the purpose in the Third Schedule of the Constitution.

It is quite clear from the content of Article 75 that in appointing the Prime Minister, the President is solely and exclusively guided by the discretion and he is not to depend on the advice of anybody. The position is different in regard to the appointment of other Ministers in the Council. For appointing the Prime Minister what guidelines are to be followed by the President are nowhere stated in the Constitution. Therefore, the President is solely to be guided by his own assessment in coming to a decision after applying his mind.

No person, including the Prime Minister, can enter upon his office unless the President administers the oath of office and of secrecy, according to the forms mentioned in the Third Schedule. It is noticed from a perusal of the Third Schedule that no separate oath of office and of secrecy is prescribed exclusively for the Prime Minister. The oaths administered to a Prime Minister and other ministers in the Union are one and the same. The Prime Minister takes the oath that he will bear true faith and allegiance to the Constitution of India, as by law established, that he will uphold the sovereignty and integrity of India, that he will faithfully and conscientiously discharge his duties as a Minister in the Union and that he will do right to all manner of people in accordance with the Constitution and the law, without fear or favour, affection or ill-will. Obviously, it is this oath of office that entitles a person to enter the office of a Prime Minister/Minister. Great sanctity has been attached to the oath to be taken before entering certain important offices like the President, Vice-President, Prime Minister under the Constitution and any violation of the oath would lead to serious consequences which, in turn, may lead to the extreme situation like removal of a person from his office.

Article 52 of the Constitution states that there shall be a President of India. Under Article 60, for a person after election to enter the office of the President, one has to take and subscribe in the presence of the Chief Justice of India an oath or an affirmation which reads as follows.

> *...will faithfully executes the office of the President ... of India and will, to the best of his ability, preserve, protect and defend the Constitution and the law and that I will devote myself to the service and wellbeing of the people of India.*

The President's oath and its significance need not be explained, since it speaks for itself. Removal of the President, which is called "impeachment" under the Constitution under Article 61 would arise where the person holding the office has violated the Constitution.. Obviously, it means the violation of the oath one has taken under the Constitution, that "he will, to the best of his ability, preserve, protect and defend the Constitution and the law and that he will devote himself to the service and wellbeing of the people."

There is significant difference between the oath of the Prime Minister and the oath of the President. While the Prime Minister takes the oath committing oneself to do right to all manner of people in accordance with the Constitution and the law, the President takes the oath to preserve, protect and defend the Constitution and the law. This means that while the Prime Minister swears to act according to the Constitution, the President swears not only to act according to the Constitution but also to prevent others from violating the Constitution and the law, for preserving, protecting and defending the same.

Therefore, the President acts as a supreme custodian of the Constitution and the interests of the People of India. He or she should not be found wanting in doing anything necessary for upholding the trust people have placed in him or her. If the President is always bound by the advice of the Prime Minister in any situation, it does not answer the reason how he or she will preserve, protect and defend the Constitution and why different oaths have been prescribed to the President and the Prime Minister. Article 53 of the Constitution categorically states that the executive power of the Union vests in the President and shall be exercised by him or her directly or through officers subordinate to him or her in accordance with this Constitution. Officers subordinate are constitutionally defined to be the Ministers of the Union. In spite of 42nd Amendment, the word "directly' in Article 53 remains intact. If, to take an extreme case, the President binds oneself by patently unconstitutional advice given by the Prime Minister and acts accordingly, notwithstanding the fact he or she acted on that advice, he would be violating the oath that he or she has taken under the Constitution and, in turn, invites oneself for impeachment under the Constitution.

New situations require new formulations and new interpretations are to be made in the interest of the country to the extent even radical interpretation and changes in the interest of the emerging nations in the 21st century. Obviously, when the Constitution expects the country having been wedded to parliamentary form of democracy, the President is assumed to play a passive role in normal circumstances, while different organs of the state function in their "defined parameters" and confrontations are resolvable by the concerned constitutional agencies. But, at the same time, the nation also expects the President to play an active role, as and when it faces political, economic or social crises, like an emergency lamp; in times of darkness, as per the mandate given by the Constitution to the President bound by the oath to preserve, protect and defend the Constitution.

I consider it a great honour for me to write a Foreword to this book, *Indian Presidency and the Successive Presidents*. Here it is relevant to mention the singular privilege I had of getting an exposure to the functioning of the office of President for a number of years since 1968.

As an Assistant Legal Adviser attached to Group (A) in the Ministry of Law, headed by the Law Secretary of the Government of India, I had the opportunity to handle the constitutional and legal issues which required advice on matters by the offices of President, Vice-President, Prime Minister and Parliament from time to time. These matters include mercy petitions, grants of pardon, State bills requiring President's assent, as well as constitutional issues raised by governors, chief ministers and other persons.

From 1968-88, for a long period of 20 years in different capacities in the Law Ministry as Deputy Additional Legal Adviser and later as Joint Additional and Special Secretary and Member-Secretary of the Law Commission of India (Secretary to GOI) I came in personal contact with President Zakir Husain and all presidents till PresidentR. Venkataraman. I handled election petitions filed in the Supreme Court challenging the election of President V.V. Giri in 1969 and also of President Fakhruddin in 1974 as an ex-officio Central Government Standing Counsel and appeared in the Supreme Court along with eminent lawyers like H.M. Seervai and Fali Nariman.

As one of the Election Commissioners, I conducted the election of President K.R. Narayanan and Vice-President Kishan Kant in the year 1997. Before their election, I had the privilege as a Law Member, with four decades of legal and constitutional background, to initiate and monitor major reforms pertaining to the election of the President and Vice-President of India, with a view to ensuring free and fair elections to the highest offices envisaged under Article 324 of the Constitution.

I may mention here that three major proposals for reforms were initiated by me as Member of the Election Commission.

In the light of past situation of the multiplicity of non-serious candidates standing for the offices of President and Vice- President it was felt essential to propose amendments in the law to ensure elimination of such frivolous candidate. For instance, at the time when Dr Zakir Husain contested for the office of President with K. Subba Rao and others in 1967, there were in all 17 candidates out of which 9 polled zeros. Similarly when V.V. Giri contested with N. Sanjeeva Reddy and others, there were 15 candidates out of which five polled zeros.

The President and Vice-President of the country are elected by the whole nation indirectly through their elected Members of Parliament and State Assemblies. The Electoral College constituted for the purpose consists currently of 776 MPs and 4120 MLAs.

The first proposal for reform, therefore, was to raise the number of proposers and seconders from 10 each to 50 to the office of President, and to raise the proposers and seconders to 20 from five each to the office of Vice-President. The second proposal was to increase the security deposit from Rs.2,500 to Rs.15,000 for the President as well as Vice-President.

If the Government were to accept the aforesaid two proposals, it was suggested by me that, in view of impending elections shortly to these two august offices, the Presidential and Vice Presidential Elections Act, 1952, may have to be amended through the proclamation of an Ordinance immediately. Here I must record my thanks to the then Prime Minister Inder Kumar Gujral, who, after considering and appreciating my proposals, got them incorporated in the Act of 1952, through proclamation of an Ordinance by President Dr Shankar Dayal Sharma.

The overwhelming impact of the aforesaid amendments was heartening to the effect that only two valid candidates were in the field for President and not more than three were there for the Vice-President in the elections in 1997, 2002 and 2007.

The third major proposal mooted then was to persuade the political parties to desist from issuing a whip to MPs and MLAs, (who got elected on their tickets) to vote to a particular candidate for the office of the President and Vice-President. This required a radical departure from the practice in the past. Democracy demands free and fair elections to all elected offices in the country from the office of President to that of Panchayat in a village. And India is essentially committed to democracy in our Constitution.

Article 21 of the Universal Declaration of Human Rights 1948 to which India was a signatory states:

> *The will of the people shall be the basis of authority of a government. This shall be expressed in periodic and genuine elections which shall be by universal and equal suffrage and shall be held by secret vote or equivalent procedure.*

Genuine elections always demand free and fair election to every elected office. As Member of the Election Commission, I was fortunate to have initiated major electoral reforms in respect of the elections to the high offices of President and Vice President. I also raised the issue of practice of issuance of a whip by political parties to MPs and MLAs, who constitute electoral college in the Presidential and Vice-Presidential elections, to cast the vote to a particular candidate. This, in my view, being a threat to the voters, came within the definition of 'undue influence' and thus militated against the spirit of democracy.

In my view, the issuance of a whip to MPs or MLAs in regard to voting for a bill or a motion on the floor of a legislature, was totally different from issuing a whip to vote in an election to the President or Vice-President. By issuance of such a whip, the parties indulged in "undue influence", such a whip being a threat to the voter with the consequences of a disciplinary action if violated, to the extent of even expulsion from the party. For ensuring free and fair elections, Section 18 of the Presidential and Vice-Presidential Act, 1952, states that there should be no 'bribery or undue influence' and for that it prescribes punishment.

The Supreme Court in the case of *V.V. Giri*, while deciding the election petition, held that MPs and MLAs were *'Independent Electors'* in the electoral college, constituted for the election in two offices.

Therefore, the office of the President or Vice-President obviously constitute choice of all people of the nation, having been elected by them (indirectly) through their elected representatives, namely MPs and MLAs representing states in the country. This means that they hold a 'Power of Attorney' as the holders of the interests of all the people in their respective constituencies. They represent the will of people in the constituencies and when they cast their vote, it means and includes the will of all the people in their constituencies who voted in their favour or against or who did not vote at all and even those people are below the age of 18 years and not qualified as voters.

Elections necessarily for offices of President and Vice-President of India are conducted as per the provisions of the Presidential and Vice-Presidential Elections Act 1952 (Act No.31 of 1952) read with Rules of 1974. As per Section 18 of that Act any use of bribery or undue influence will be GROUND TO DECLARE THE ELECTION OF THE RETURNED CANDIDATE VOID.

To explain further, sub-section 2 of Section 18 specifically states that 'bribery and undue influence' will have the same meaning as in Chapter IX A of the Indian Penal Code, 1860 (sections A-H). "Bribery" and "Undue Influence", as defined in Sections 171-B & C, are made punishable with "one year imprisonment and fine or both" as per Sections 171 E&F.

Concerning "Undue Influence" the Supreme Court of India clearly defined and interpreted it in the case of *Shiv Prasad Singh* vs *V.V. Giri* (1970 2 SCC 567). Undue Influence at an election is defined as the voluntary interference or attempted interference with the right of any person to stand, or not to stand, or withdraw from being a candidate, or to vote or refrain from voting. This covers all threats of injury to person or property and illegal methods of persuasion and any interference with the liberty of the candidates or electors ... The expression 'free exercise of the electoral right" does not mean that a voter is not to be influenced ... in the context of an election in a democratic society and the candidates and their supporters must naturally be allowed to canvass support by all legal legitimate means (Rattan Lal and Dhirajlal, *The Indian Penal Code*, 1983, p.139).

Political parties deserve high compliments for their foresight and wisdom to have accepted unanimously my constitutional interpretation of "issuance of a whip" in the electors to the offices of the President and the Vice-President, which is a radical departure from the past and who did not issue any whip during 1997, 2002, 2007, and 2012 elections.

Thus, the political parties heavily contributed in holding free and fair elections to apex offices and thereby catapulted Indian democracy to greatest heights in the comity of world nations.

I am happy that M.L Ahuja, who is the author of this book, has been a discerning thinker and writer, apart from earlier being the Area Representative of the International Association of Oriental Librarians and the Executive Secretary of Afro-Asian Book Council. He has rightly chosen the subject of all Indian Presidents and their roles from 1952 till date in the country. The thumb-line sketches of all the distinguished Presidents of this country, including Dr Rajendra Prasaad, Dr Zakir Husain, Dr S. Radhakrishnan, V.V. Giri, Fakhruddin

Ali Ahmed, Neelam Sanjiva Reddy, Giani Zail Singh, R. Venkataraman, Dr S.D. Sharma, K.R. Narayanan, Dr A.P.J. Abdul Kalam, Pratibha Devisingh Patil and Pranab Mukherjee would be a welcome addition to the existing literature on the subject.

The book is not only a ready reference of the biographical profiles of all the Presidents in India since Independence but also amply throws light on the way these Indian Presidents tackled difficult situations in difficult times and proved themselves to be beacon lights and upholders of Indian Constitution in the service of the Indian people since the formation of the Republic.

I am sure, this book will be welcomed by institutions, libraries, public at large and democracies abroad too. The author, M.L. Ahuja, deserves all encomiums for the sincere and hard work in bringing out this book.

Long live Democracy.

(Dr GVG Krishnamurty)
New Delhi
July 25, 2012

Preface

In June-July 2012, it was for the second time in Independent India that election for the President of India gained political significance. First time it was in 1964 when Indira Gandhi used the presidential election to consolidate her hold over the Congress. She then put up Vice President V.V. Giri as an alternative candidate to the Congress party's official candidate, Neelam Sanjiva Reddy. Giri defeated Reddy in a close contest.

The situation in 2012 had been altogether different as compared to all the previous presidential elections. In 2007, the Congress President, Sonia Gandhi could easily pull the obscure Pratibha Patil at the last minute without any difficulty and with no dissent from her own party or any coalition partner. In 2012, Sonia had to face troublesome allies and there was no clear consensus in the Congress Party. Sonia's choice had been limited, especially when Mamta Banerjee of Trinamool Congress and Mulayam Singh Yadav drove a hard bargain with the Congress. Both wanted generous financial grants from the Centre for their states in return for their assured support. It wasn't easy for the Congress to oblige them.

The only way for Sonia was to make Pranab Mukherjee her choice. Mukherjee had been the Congress Party's undisputed candidate. It was calculated that out of a total number of 10,98,882 votes (5,49,408 of MPs and 5,49,474 of MLAs) the winner needed at least 5,49,442 votes. UPA (Congress+ TMC+DMK+NCP+Allied) had 4,46,345 (41 per cent). NDA (BJP+JDU+SAD+SS) had 3,04,785 votes. Non-UPA/Non-ND had 2,62,408 (24 per cent), small parties had 71,498 (6%). SP+TMC had 116,658 votes (6+4%), BSP+BJD+JD(U) had 114,993 votes (4%+4%+3%). Ultimately, UPA's strategy worked well and its nominee, Pranab Mukherjee, emerged successful with an overwhelming majority.

The emerging scenario requires presidency in India to be redefined. The President in India needs to be interactive. But

The President has to work within some parameters. What are those parameters? I have tried to analyze them in Part I of the book and Part II describes the roles each one of these presidents during their tenure since Independence. Again, not many people know the process involved in the presidential election. It is not like Assembly or Lok Sabha election. The process of election petition, in this case, is also different. The reader will find two separate chapters dealing with these aspects.

I have tried to make the book useful for the students of politics, journalists, and discriminative readers. Dr GVG Krishnamurty, former Election Commissioner of India with rich experience in the study of constitutional law, has been kind enough to contribute his scholarly Foreword. I know Dr Krishnamurty ever since 1968 when he was legal advisolr in the Ministry of Law, Government of India, looking after the legal issues concerning the President and Vice President of India. With this vast experience his Foreword reflects his erudition and pragmatic approach. In view of this, this Foreword should certainly add value to this book. I would like to express my deep sense of gratitude to him for sparing his valuable time. I am thankful to Mr T. Lokanadham, Mr Mukesh Sharma and many others who were involved in designing the layout and cover of this book. I am thankful to Mr Surjeet Khurana of Synergy Books India for getting this book published within a short span of time. I hope his publishing house will be able to penetrate the market and make this book accessible to the people at large. My thanks are also due to my wife, Mrs Asha Ahuja, who assisted me in every way while I concentrated on preparing this manuscript.

M.L Ahuja
July 29, 2012

Contents

Foreword iv
Preface xvii

Part I
Indian Presidency

1. President in the Indian Constitution 2
2. President vs Prime Minister and Council of Ministers 27
3. Procedure for Election 35
4. Election Petition 45

Part II
Sucessive Presidents

5. Rajendra Prasad 55
6. Sarvepalli Radhakrishnan 67
7. Zakir Husain 77
8. Justice Mohammed Hidayatullah 87
9. Varahagiri Venkata Giri 99
10. Fakhruddin Ali Ahmed 109
11. Basappa Danappa Jatti 117
12. Neelam Sanjiva Reddy 119
13. Giani Zail Singh 131
14. Ramaswami Venkataraman 147
15. Shankar Dayal Sharma 157
16. K. R. Narayanan 167
17. A.P.J. Abdul Kalam 179
18. Pratibha Devisingh Patil 195
19. Pranab Mukherjee 205

Part III
Appendix

Excerpts from President Pranab Mukherjee's Address to the Nation on the eve of 66th Independence Day. 217

Part I

Indian Presidency

1

President in the Indian Constitution

The President of India is the head of state of the Republic of India. The president is the formal head of the Legislature, Executive and Judiciary and is the commander-in-chief of the Indian Armed Forces. The power to pardon and clemency vests with the President of India.

Part V, Chapter 1 of the Constitution deals with the Executive of the Union. Article 52 states that there shall be a President of India. Article 54 defines how the President should be elected. It states that the President shall be elected by the members of an electoral consisting of

A. The elected members of both Houses of Parliament; and

B. The elected members of the Legislative Assemblies of the States.

Article 52 to 62 deal with the manner of election, his term, eligibility, qualifications, conditions, oath, impeachment and time for holding an election to fill a vacancy in the office of the President. The President is conferred with various categories of powers—executive, legislative, judicial, military, ordinance-making and emergency power.

Qualification

Article 58 of the Constitution sets the principle qualifications one must meet to be eligible to the office of the President. A President must be

- a citizen of India;
- of 35 years of age or above;
- qualified to become a member of the Lok Sabha; and
- the Constitution of India is silent about the candidate contesting again in the election (Article 53).

A person shall not be eligible for election as President if he/she holds any office of profit under the Government of India or the Government of any State or under any local or other authority subject to the control of any of the said governments.

- Certain office-holders, however, are permitted to stand as Presidential candidates. These are:
- The current Vice President;
- The Governor of any State;
- A Minister of the Union or of any State including Prime Minister and Chief Ministers.

In the event that the Vice President, a State Governor or a Minister is elected President, they are considered to have vacated their previous office on the date they begin serving as President.

Certain conditions, as per Article 59 of the Constitution, debar any eligible citizen from contesting the presidential elections. The conditions are:

- The President shall not be a member of either House of Parliament or of a House of the Legislature of any State, and if a member of either House of Parliament or of a House of the Legislature of any State be elected President, he shall be deemed to have vacated his seat in that House on the date on which he enters upon his office as President.
- The President shall not hold any other office of profit.
- The President shall be entitled, without payment of rent, to the use of his official residences and shall also be entitled to such emoluments, allowances and privileges as may be determined by Parliament by law and until provision in that behalf is so made, such emoluments, allowances and privileges, as are specified in the Second Schedule.
- The emoluments and allowances of the President shall not be diminished during his term of office.Whenever the office becomes vacant, the new President is chosen by an electoral college consisting of the elected members of both houses of Parliament, the elected members of the State Legislative Assemblies (Vidhan Sabha) and the elected members of the legislative assemblies of the Union Territories of Delhi and Puducherry.

The nomination of a candidate for election to the office of the President must be subscribed by at least 50 electors as proposers and 50 electors as seconders. Each candidate has to make a security deposit of Rs.15,000 in the Reserve Bank of India. The security deposit is liable to be forfeited in case the candidate fails to secure one-sixth of the votes polled.

Election

The President is elected from a group of nominees by the elected members of the Parliament of India (Lok Sabha and Rajya Sabha) as well as of the state legislatures (Vidhan Sabhas), and serves for a term of five years. The elction is conducted by the Election Commission of India. Historically, ruling party (majority in the Lok Sabha) nominees have been elected and run largely uncontested. Incumbents are permitted to stand for re-election. A formula is used to allocate votes. Thus, there is a balance between the population of each state and the number of votes assembly members from a state can cast, and to give an equal balance between State Assembly members and National parliament members. If no candidate receives a majority of votes, then there is a system by which losing candidates are eliminated from the contest and their votes are transferred to other candidates, until one gains a majority. The Vice-President is elected by a direct vote of all members (elected and nominated) of the Lok Sabha and Rajya Sabha.

In this way, the President of India is elected by indirect election that is by an electoral college, in accordance with the system of proportional representation by means of the single transferable vote.

The Electoral College shall consist of

1. The elected members of both Houses of Parliament;
2. The elected members of the legislative assemblies of the States; and
3. The elected members of the Union Territories of Delhi and Puducherry (Pondicherry);

A person who holds or who has held the office of a President is eligible for re-election to that office. Article 68 clearly explains how a vacancy in the office of the President be filled: (1) An election to fill a vacancy caused by the expiration of the term of office of Vice-President shall be completed before the expiration of the term. (2) An election to fill a vacancy in the office of Vice-President occurring by reason of his death, resignation or removal, or otherwise shall be held as soon as possible after the occurrence of the vacancy, and the person elected to fill the vacancy shall, subject to the provisions of Article 67, be entitled to hold office for the full term of five years from the date on which he/she enters upon his/her office."

Each elector casts a different number of votes. The general principle is that the total number of votes cast by Members of Parliament equals the total number of votes cast by State Legislators. Also, legislators from larger states cast more votes than those from smaller states. Finally, the number of legislators in a state matters; if a state has few legislators, then each legislator has more votes; if a state has many legislators, then each legislator has fewer votes.

The actual calculation for votes cast by a particular state is calculated by dividing the state's population by 1000, which is divided again by the number of legislators from the State voting in the electoral college. This number is the number of votes per legislator in a given state. For votes cast by those in Parliament, the total number of votes cast by all state legislators is divided by the number of members of both Houses of Parliament. This is the number of votes per member of either house of Parliament.

In 2007, the President of India was elected indirectly by the members of the Indian Parliament and by the individual States' Legislative Assemblies. Although Indian presidential elections involve actual voting by MPs and MLAs, they tend to vote for the candidate supported by their respective parties.

Hence, the internal process for the election involved lobbying by parties for their respective candidates. UPA, the ruling coalition and NDA, the major opposition coalition hence hold the key to the nomination and support gathering. Another key player in the final decision was the Left parties, which agreed to support the UPA candidate under certain conditions for nomination. Mayawati, the former chief minister of Uttar Pradesh, the most populous state of India, was also said to be a significant factor in the final election.

The oath of office of the President is administered by the Chief Justice of India and in his absence, the senior most Judge of the Supreme Court available. It is as follows:

> *I, (name), do swear in the name of God (or solemnly affirm) that I will faithfully execute the office of President (or discharge the functions of the President) of the Republic of India, and will to the best of my ability preserve, protect and defend the Constitution and the law, and that I will devote myself to the service and well-being of the people of Republic of India.*

Anti defection laws are not applicable for voting in Presidential elections. Members of the electoral college are free to vote according to their conscience and are not bound to follow party whip. Since the election is by secret voting, political parties cannot identify the voting patterns easily.

But a sitting President or Vice President of the Union or the Governor of any State or a Minister either for the Union or for any State is not disqualified for election as President [Article 58].

Term of Office

The President holds office for a term of five years. However he can resign from his office at any time by addressing the resignation letter to the Vice President. Any resignation addressed to the Vice President shall forthwith be communicated to the Speaker of the Lok Sabha[Article 56, 57]

Emoluments

The President of India used to receive Rs.10,000 (US$ 200) per month as per the Constitution. This amount was increased to Rs.50,000 (US$ 1,000) in 1998. On September 11, 2008 the Government of India increased the salary of the President to 150,000 (US$ 3,000). However, almost everything that the President does or wants to do is taken care of by the annual Rs.22.5 crore (approx. US$ 5 million) budget that the Government allots for his or her upkeep.

The Rashtrapati Bhavan in New Delhi is the official residence. It is the largest Presidential Palace in the world. The Rashtrapati Nilayam at Bolarum, Secunderabad and Retreat Building at Chharabra, Shimla, are the official Retreat Residents of the President of India. The official state car of the President is a custom-built heavily armoured Mercedes Benz S600 (W221) Pullman Guard.

Removal

The President may be removed before the expiry of his/her term through impeachment. A President can be removed for violation of the Constitution of India [Article 61(1)]

The process may start in either of the two houses of the Parliament. The house initiates the process by levelling the charges against the President. The charges are contained in a notice which has to be signed by at least one quarter of the total members of that house. The notice is sent to the President and 14 days later it is taken up for consideration.

A resolution to impeach the President has to be passed by a two-third majority of the total members of the originating house. It is then sent to the other house. The other house investigates the charges that have been made. During this process, the President has the right to defend himself/herself through an authorized counsel. If the second house also approves the charges made by two-third majority again, the President stands impeached and is deemed to have vacated his/her office from the date when such a resolution stands passed. Other than impeachment, no other penalty can be given to the President for the violation of the Constitution.

No President in India has faced impeachment proceedings since Independence. Hence, the above provisions have never been used.

Filling Up the Vacancy

In the event of a vacancy created for the President's post due to death, resignation, removal, etc., Article 65 of the Indian Constitution says that the Vice President will have to discharge his duties. The Vice President reverts to his office when a new President is elected and enters upon his office. When the President is unable to act owing to his absence, illness or any other cause, the Vice President discharges the President's functions for a temporary period until the President resumes his/her duties.

When the Vice President acts as, or discharges the functions of the President, he/she has all the powers and immunities of the President and is entitled to the same emoluments as the President.

Parliament has, by an enactment, made provision for the discharge of the functions of the President when vacancies occur in the offices of the President and of the Vice President simultaneously, owing to removal, death, resignation of the incumbent or otherwise. In such an eventuality, the Chief Justice, or in his absence, the senior most Judge of the Supreme Court of India available discharges the functions of the President until a newly elected President enters upon his/her office or a newly elected Vice President begins to act as President under Article 65 of the Constitution, whichever is the earlier.

Powers

Article 53 (1) of the Constitution vests in the President "the executive power of the Union" to be "exercised by him/her either directly or through officers subordinate to him/her" in accordance with the provisions of the Constitution. However, the Constitution also states that the Council of Ministers, headed by the Prime Minister, is "to aid and advise the President who shall, in the exercise of his functions, act in accordance with such advice".

However, the Article 74 (2) bars all courts completely from assuming even an existence of such an advice. Therefore, from the court's point of view, the real executive power lies with the President. As far as President's decision and action are concerned no one can challenge such decision or action on the ground that it is not in accordance with the advice tendered by the Ministers or that it is based on no advice. However, the President has the following powers to be exercised with the aid of the Council of Ministers.:

Power to Pardon

As mentioned in Article 72 of Indian Constitution, the President is empowered with the powers to grant pardons in the following situations:

- Punishment is for offence against Union Law;
- Punishment is by a Military Court; and
- Sentence is a death sentence.

The President of India can grant a pardon or reduce the sentence of a convicted person, particularly in cases involving capital punishment. A similar and parallel power vests in the Governors of each State under Article 161.

However, it is important to note that India has a unitary structure of government and there is no body of state law. All crimes are crimes against the Union of India. Therefore, a convention has developed that the Governor's powers is exercised for only minor offenses, while requests for pardons and reprieves for major offenses and offenses committed in the Union Territories are deferred to the President.

Both the President and Governor are bound by the advice of their respective Councils of Ministers and hence the exercise of this power is of an executive character. It is, therefore, subject to judicial review (*Maru Ram v Union of India*, confirmed by *Kehar Singh vs Union of India*,1989). It also depends upon other provisions of law, i.e. sections 54 and 55 of the Indian Penal Code, Sections 432,433 and 433A of the Criminal Procedure Code of the Indian criminal justice system and also the sentencing policies of state. ("the power under articles 72 /161.... is absolute and cannot be fettered by any.)

The purpose of clemency was to add a humane approach by means of a reprieve or mercy. Forgiveness is considered to be divine. In matters pertaining to public welfare it becomes necessary to see whether granting pardon overturns the intention of the conviction.

The Constitution of India permits any convict, who is sentenced to death, to appeal for mercy. However, the President and the Governors are not obliged to accept every mercy plea. They are supposed to take their decisions on the basis of the advice given by the cabinet.

According to the Constitution of India, the President and the Governors of State are bound to act on the advice of the Union council of ministers while deciding on mercy petitions. The exercise of these powers can be granted under Articles 72 and 161, but they are subject to judicial review. However, the scope of this judicial review is limited to examining whether the clemency powers have been used with reasonable application of mind or on the basis of extraneous or malafide consideration.

When a decision is made on application of mind, the court will take no action over it but if the pardon appears to be based on malafide or extraneous considerations, it can set aside the decision of the President or the Governor.

A clear instance of this principle was evident in a court judgment that set aside the decision of Andhra Pradesh Governor, Sushil Kumar Shinde, to remit the sentence of a Congress activist, Gouru Venkata Reddy. Reddy was undergoing a ten-year prison sentence for killing two persons including a TDP activist.

The Constitution of India mandates that the rule of law is essential for all considerations. When the President or Governor considers the mercy petition or clemency petition on the basis of caste, religion or political loyalty, it becomes a case of extraneous consideration. The President and the Governors can also exercise their power to pardon on the ground that they do not feel justice was done or the sentence passed by the court is too harsh.

The Supreme Court, in one of its judgments, stated: It can no longer be said that prerogative power is *ipso facto* immune from judicial review. An undue exercise of this power is to be deplored. Considerations of religion, caste or political loyalty are irrelevant and fraught with discrimination. These are prohibited grounds. Rule of law is the basis for evaluation of all decisions. Thus, the President and the Governors of state can grant pardon or reprieves based on the rule of law and not any other consideration.

In 2012, President Pratibha Patil commuted death sentence of some convicts on the recommendation of former Home Minister P. Chittambaran leaving nine others. On August 17,

2012, after President Pranab Mukherjee took over, 14 ex-judges of the Supreme Court sent signed letters requesting him to turn the capital punishment of the convicts into life sentence. They pointed out that the death sentence to these nine persons by various two-judge benches of the Supreme Court were "contrary to the binding dictum of rarest of rare" pronouncement in the 1980 five-judge bench verdict in *Bachan Singh* vs *State of Punjab*. The Bachan Singh prescription of weighing the circumstances relating to "the crime as well as the criminal" before pronouncing a death penalty was disregarded for the first time in 1995 in *Ravji Ram Chandra* vs *State of Rajasthan* where a two-judge bench ruled that it was "the nature and gravity of the crime but not the criminal, which are germane for consideration of appropriate punishment in a criminal trial." The Ravji approach of focussing on the aggravating circumstances (namely the crime) at the expense of the mitigating circumstances (namely the criminal), it was stated, served as a precedent to at least six judgments leading to the hanging of Ravji in 1996 and Surja Ram the following year. The erosion of the rarest of rare doctrine was finally decried by the Supreme Court in 2009 in *Santosh Bariyar* vs *State of Maharashtra* followed by two more such corrections in 2010 and 2011.

In their appeals, the retired judges took pain to clarify that none of the cases in question involved crimes against the state. Further, the concerns raised in their appeals, it was stated, have nothing to do with the larger debate about the desirability or retaining the death sentence. "Rather they pertain to the administration of the death penalty in a conscientious, fair and just manner," It was further stated that "executions of persons wrongly sentenced to death will severely undermine the credibility of the criminal justice system. It was pointed out that this matter goes to the very heart of our Constitution because it involves the taking of lives by the state on the basis of judgments admitted to be erroneous by the Supreme Court.

Diplomatic Powers

All international treaties and agreements are negotiated and concluded on behalf of the President. However, in practice, such negotiations are usually carried out by the Prime Minister along with his Cabinet (especially the Foreign Minister). Also, such treaties are subject to the approval of the Parliament. The President represents India in international forums and affairs where such a function is chiefly ceremonial. The President may also send and receive diplomats, i.e. the officers from the Indian Foreign Service. The President is the first person of the country.

Military Powers

The President is the supreme commander of the defence forces of India. The President can declare war or conclude peace, subject to the approval of Parliament only under the decision of the Council of the Armed Forces Chief staffs, Military Secretary and President's Officer. All important treaties and contracts are made in president's name.

Emergency Powers

The President can declare three types of emergencies: national, state and financial.

(i) *National Emergency*

National emergency is caused by war, external aggression or armed rebellion in the whole of India or a part of its territory. Such an emergency was declared in India in 1962 (Indo-China war), 1971 (Indo-Pakistan war), 1975 to 1977 (declared by Indira Gandhi on account of "internal disturbance").

Under Article 352 of the Indian Constitution, the President can declare such an emergency only on the basis of a written request by the Cabinet Ministers headed by the Prime Minister. Such a proclamation must be approved by the Parliament within one month. Such an emergency can be imposed for six months. It can be extended by six months by repeated parliamentary approval, up to a maximum of three years.

In such an emergency, Fundamental Rights of Indian citizens can be suspended. The six freedoms under Right to Freedom are automatically suspended. However, the Right to Life and Personal Liberty cannot be suspended (Article 21).

The Parliament can make laws on the 66 subjects of the State List which contains subjects on which the state governments can make laws. Also, all money bills are referred to the Parliament for its approval. The term of the Lok Sabha can be extended by a period of up to one year, but not so as to extend the term of Parliament beyond six months after the end of the declared emergency.

(ii) *State Emergency*

State emergency, also known as President's Rule, is declared due to breakdown of constitutional machinery in a state.

If the President is satisfied, on the basis of the report of the Governor of the concerned state or from other sources that the governance in a state cannot be carried out according to the provisions in the Constitution, he/she can declare a state of emergency in the state. Such an emergency must be approved by the Parliament within a period of two months.

Under Article 356 of the Indian Constitution, it can be imposed from six months to a maximum period of three years with repeated parliamentary approval every six months. If the emergency needs to be extended for more than three years, this can be achieved by a constitutional amendment, as has happened in Punjab and Jammu and Kashmir.

During such an emergency, the President can take over the entire work of the executive, and the Governor administers the state in the name of the President. The Legislative Assembly can be dissolved or may remain in suspended animation. The Parliament makes laws on the 66 subjects of the state list. All money bills have to be referred to the Parliament for approval.

A State Emergency can be imposed via the following:

1. By Article 356 – If that state failed to run constitutionally, i.e. constitutional machinery has failed; and
2. By Article 365 – If that state is not working according to the given direction of the Union Government.

This type of emergency needs the approval of the Parliament within two months. This type of emergency can last up to a maximum of three years via extensions after each six month period. However, after one year it can be extended only if

1. A state of National Emergency has been declared in the country or in the particular state; and
2. The Election Commission finds it difficult to organize an election in that state.

However, the Governor of any State does'nt have the unbridled power. On March 6, 2005, for instance, the Governor of Bihar sent report to the President of India recommending 'newly-constituted Assembly' to be kept in suspended animation for the present, without summoning the Assembly for the purpose of getting oath of successful members under Article 188 & Para VII A & B. In his report, the Governor apprehended 'horse trading'. The report of the Governor was received by Union of India on May 22, 2005 and, on the same day, the Union Cabinet met at about 11 pm, and decided to accept the report of the Governor and sent a fax message to the President of India, who had already left for Moscow, recommending the dissolution of the Legislative Assembly of Bihar. The President of India received the message at his Camp office in Moscow at 0152 hrs (IST). The President of India accorded his approval and sent the same through the fax message, which was received at 0350 hrs (IST) on May 23, 2005. After due process, the notification was issued formally at 1430 hrs (IST) in May 2005 dissolving the Bihar Assembly.

Article 356 (1) of the Constitution states that on receipt of report from the Governor of the State or otherwise, if the President is satisfied that a situation has arisen in which the Government of the State cannot be carried on in accordance with the provisions of the Constitution, he may, by Proclamation, assume to himself all or any of the functions of the Government of the State and all or any of the powers vested in or exercisable by the Governor or any body or authority in the State other than the Legislature of the State. He can declare that the powers of the Legislature of the State shall be exercisable by or under the authority of Parliament. He can make such incidental and consequential provisions as appear to the President to be necessary or desirable for giving effect to the objects of the Proclamation, including provisions for suspending in whole or in part of the operation of any provision of the Constitution relating to any body or authority in the State.

Power under Article 356(1) is an emergency power and it is not an absolute power. The Supreme Court stated that emergency means a situation, which is not normal, a situation that calls for urgent remedial action. Article 356 confers a power to be exercised by the President in exceptional circumstances to discharge the obligation cast upon him by Article 355. It is a measure to protect and preserve the Constitution. The Governor takes the oath, prescribed by Article 159 to preserve, protect and defend the Constitution and the laws to the best of his ability. Power under Article 356 is conditional, condition being formation of satisfaction of the President as contemplated by Article 356 (1). The satisfaction of the President is the satisfaction of Council of Ministers. As provided in Article 74(1), the President acts on the aid and advice of the Council of Ministers. The Court is debarred from inquiring into such advice. However, it has been held in *Bommai's case* that "it does not bar scrutiny of the material on the basis of which the advice is given." Clause (2) of Article 74 cannot be read or understood as conferring an immunity upon the Council of Ministers to explain, defend and justify the orders and acts of the President done in exercise of his functions. The limited provision contained in Article 74(2) cannot override the basic provisions in the Constitution relating to judicial review.

The nine-Judge Bench in *Bommai's case* considered the validity of dissolution of Legislative Assembly of States of Karnataka, Meghalaya, Nagaland, Madhya Pradesh, Himachal Pradesh and Rajasthan. It is important to note that in Bommai's case the Supreme Court was concerned with cases of dissolution of assemblies when cabinets were in office. It was held that Article 356(1) is subject to judicial review at least to the extent of examining whether the conditions precedent to the issue of Proclamation have been satisfied or not. This examination will necessarily involve the scrutiny as to whether there existed material for the satisfaction of the President that the situation had arisen in which the Government of the State could not be carried on in accordance with the provisions of the Constitution. While considering the question of material, it was held that it is not the personal whim, wish, view or opinion of or the *ipse dixit* of the President *de hors* the material but a legitimate inference drawn from the material placed before him which is relevant for the purpose. In other words, the President has to be convinced of or has to have sufficient information and proof with regard to or has to be free from doubt or uncertainty about the state of things indicating that the situation in question has arisen. Therefore, though the sufficiency or otherwise of the material cannot be questioned, the legitimacy of inference drawn from material is certainly open to judicial review.

It has been further held that when the Proclamation is challenged, the burden would be on the Union Government to satisfy that there exists material, which showed that the Government could not be carried on in accordance with the provisions of the Constitution. Since such material would be exclusively within the knowledge of the Union Government in view of the provisions of Section 106 of the Evidence Act, the burden of proof would be on the Union Government. In view of this, the report on the basis whereof Proclamation dissolving the Assembly of Karnataka had been issued was subjected to a close scrutiny.

The Supreme Court observed that in the case of 2005 Bihar Assembly dissolution, there cannot be any presumption of allurement or horse trading only for the reason that some MLAs expressed the view which was opposed to the public posture of their leader and decided to support the formation of the Government by the leader of another political party. Bihar Assembly dissolution was stated to be different from the dissolution of assemblies of Madhya Pradesh, Rajasthan and Himachal Pradesh, where it was held in *Bommai's case* that the reports of the Governors disclosed that the State Governments had miserably failed to protect the citizens and property of the State against internal disturbances. In such cases, from the Governor's reports it was found that the reports were based on relevant material and were bona fide and after due verification.

In view of this, the Court has the power to examine the material facts. The Judges in the Supreme Court observed in Bihar Assembly case that the Court cannot remain a silent spectator watching the subversion of the Constitution. They also observed that "in the facts and circumstances of this case, the Governor may be the main player, but Council of Ministers should have verified facts stated in the report of the Governor before hurriedly accepting it as a gospel truth as to what Governor stated. Clearly, the Governor has misled the Council of Ministers, which lead to aid and advice being given by the Council of Ministers to the President leading to the issue of the impugned Proclamation."

Immunity to the Governor

Can there be any immunity to the Governor? In an order dated September 8, 2005, the Supreme Court had held that the Constitution of India grants immunity to the Governor as provided in Article 361 of the Constitution. Article 361(1), *inter alia*, provides that the Governor shall not be answerable to any Court for the exercise and performance of the powers and duties of his office or for any act done or purported to be done by him in the exercise and performance of those powers and duties. However, in its verdict in *Rameshwar Prasad & Ors.* Vs *Union of India & Anr* (2006) the Supreme Court further observed that the immunity granted does not affect the power of this Court to judicially scrutinize attack made on the Proclamation issued under Article 356(1) of the Constitution of India on the ground of *mala fides* or it being *ultra vires* and that it would be for the Government to satisfy the court and adequately meet such ground of challenge.

It was held that a *mala fide* act is wholly outside the scope of the power and has no existence in the eyes of the law. It was also held that the expression 'purported to be done' in Article 361 does not cover acts which are *mala fide* or *ultra vires* and thus Government supporting the Proclamation under Article 356(1) shall have to meet the challenge. The immunity granted under Article 361 does not mean that the grounds of *mala fide* or being *ultra vires* would not be examined by the Court.

On January 19, 2009, President's rule was imposed on the Indian State of Jharkhand, making it the latest state where this kind of emergency has been imposed.

(iii) *Financial Emergency*

If the President is satisfied that there is an economic situation in which the financial stability or credit of India is threatened, he/she can proclaim financial emergency as per the Article 360 of the Constitution. Such an emergency must be approved by the Parliament within two months. It has never been declared. On an occasion, the financial stability or credit of India has indeed been threatened, but a financial emergency was avoided through the selling off of India's gold reserves.

A state of financial emergency remains in force indefinitely until revoked by the President.

The President can reduce the salaries of all government officials, including judges of the Supreme Court and High Courts, in case of a financial emergency. All money bills passed by the State legislatures are submitted to the President for approval. They can direct the state to observe certain principles (economy measures) relating to financial matters.

Election Petition

According to Article 71 of the Constitution of India, all doubts and disputes arising out of or in connection with the election of a President or Vice-President shall be enquired into and decided by the Supreme Court. Further, as per Section 14 of the Presidential and Vice-Presidential Elections Act, 1952, an election petition can be filed before the Supreme Court. For the sake of clarity it should be worthwhile giving below the relevant excerpts of the Supreme Court cases and the issues involved.

In *Charan Lal Sahu & Others* vs *Giani Zail Singh & Another 1984* AIR 304, 1984 SCR (2) 6, the question was raised about the maintainability of petitions. It was contended that neither of the two petitioners was a 'candidate' within the meaning of Section 13(a) of the Presidential and Vice-Presidential Elections Act, 1952 and since under Section 14A, an election petition can be filed only by a person who was a candidate at the election, the petitioners had no standing to file the petitions. In this case, the Returning Officer accepted the nomination papers of two candidates only, viz. Giani Zail Singh and Justice

H.R. Khanna. The election was held on July 12, 1982, and Giani Zail Singh was declared as the successful candidate. The petitioners who had filed their nomination papers contested the election on various grounds and alleged that Giani Zail Singh exercised undue influence over the voters through his confidants.

The second case worth mentioning is *Kirpal Singh* vs *V.V. Giri*, 1970 AIR 2097, 1971 SCR (2) 197. Four election petitions filed under Section 14 of the Presidential and Vice-Presidential Election Act of 1952 and Article 71 of the Constitution of India challenged the election of V. V. Giri to the office of the President of India. The petitioner Shiv Kirpal Singh was a candidate in the election and so was the other person. The nominations of both these petitioners were rejected by the Returning Officer.

The main question that came up for consideration was whether the distribution of an anonymous pamphlet making defamatory statements about one of the candidates at the election, in the manner alleged by the petitioners, amounted to exercise of undue influence within the meaning of Section 18 of the Presidential and Vice-Presidential Election Act 31 of 1952 read with Secstion 171 C of the Indian Penal Code. Though the fact that who got the pamphlet published and distributed could not be established it held that the argument completely disregards the structure and provisions of Section 171C. The Section is enacted in three parts. The first stage contains the definition of undue influence. This is in wide terms and renders a person voluntarily interfering or attempting to interfere with the free exercise of any electoral right guilty of committing undue influence. That this is very wide is indicated by the opening sentence of sub-section (2) that is, "without prejudice to the generality of the provisions of sub-section (1)". It is well settled that when the expression is used anything contained in the provisions following this expression is not intended to cut down the generality of the meaning of the preceding provision. It proceeds on the assumption that a declaration of public policy or a promise of public action or the mere exercise of a legal right can interfere with an electoral right, and therefore it provides that if there is no intention to interfere with the electoral right it shall not be deemed to be interference within the meaning of this section. Such a declaration of public policy or the promise of public action can only act and tend to interfere at the stage when a voter is trying to make up his mind as to which candidate he would support.

The expression "free exercise of the electoral right" does not mean that a voter is not to be influenced. This expression has to be read in the context of an election in a democratic society and the candidates and their supporters must naturally be allowed to canvass support by all legal and legitimate means. This exercise of the right by a candidate or his supporters to canvass support does not interfere or attempt to interfere with the free exercise of the electoral right. What does however attempt to interfere with the exercise of an electoral right is "tyranny over the mind". If the contention of the respondent was to be accepted it would be quite legitimate on the part of the candidate or his supporters to hypnotise a voter and then send him to vote. At the stage of casting his ballot paper there would be no pressure cast on him because his mind has already been made up for him by the hypnotiser.

On the evidence in the case, the Supreme Court held that the pamphlet in question was distributed by post and in the Central Hall of Parliament by some members of Parliament and there was wide discussion about it in the Central Hall. The allegations in the pamphlet, made against one of the losing candidates were covered under Section 171C I.P.C. The argument that the pamphlet could not come under Section 171C because it was anonymously distributed was considered as fallacious. A series of anonymous attempts in a country like ours, it was stated, would have as much, if not more, effect as one open powerful attempt. It would be dangerous to provide a sanctuary for anonymous attempts. Moreover, when Members of Parliament distribute a pamphlet in the Central Hall it has the same effect as if they had endorsed the pamphlet in writing.

Accordingly, it was held that the distribution of the pamphlet by post as also distribution in the Central Hall constituted an attempt to interfere with the free exercise of the right of vote within Section 18 of the Act. There was however no evidence to show that the respondent had any connection with the pamphlet or with its distribution. Nor was there any evidence to show that anyone connected with the distribution either through the post or in the Central Hall had any contact with the respondent, or that he distributed it with his knowledge or connivance.

It is well settled that the burden of proving that the result of the election has been materially affected is on the petitioners. As held by this Court in *Samant N. Balkrishna* v. *George Fernandes*, the matter cannot be decided on possibility or reasonable judicial guess. On the evidence in the present case it was difficult to hold that the petitioners had proved that the publication and distribution of the pamphlet materially affected the result of the election. It only leads to the conclusion that it probably did have some effect but the vast majority of the electors were able to throw off the effect of the pamphlet and vote according to their own personal wish or according to the mandate of their party.

Justice Bhargava held that sub-section (1) of Section 171C in general terms makes any act an 'undue influence' if it interferes or attempts to interfere with the free exercise of any electoral right and if it is committed voluntarily. The electoral right, according to the definition in Section 171A(b) is the right of a voter to vote or refrain from voting. Undue influence can be held to be committed if the person charged with the offence interferes or attempts to interfere with the free exercise of this right of voting or refraining from voting. When an elector exercises the right of voting it can be envisaged that he goes through the mental process of first taking a decision that he will vote in favour of a particular candidate and thereafter, having made up his mind, he has to go and exercise that electoral right by casting the vote in favour of the candidate chosen by him. The language used in Section 171C indicates that the offence of undue influence comes in at the second stage when the offender interferes or attempts to interfere with the free exercise of that choice of voting in accordance with the decision already taken by the voter. It, therefore, follows that if any acts are done which merely influence the voter in making his choice between one candidate or another, they will not amount to interference with the free exercise of the electoral right. In fact, all canvassing that is carried on and which is considered legitimate is intended to influence the choice of a voter at the first stage and that is quite permissible. Once the choice has been made by the voter, there should be no interference with the free exercise by him of that choice by actually casting the vote, or in the alternative there may be cases where a voter may decide that he will not vote for any candidate at all but some acts are done which compel him to cast his vote. It is in such cases that the offence of undue influence will be held to have been committed.

The language used in the definition of undue influence implies that an offence of undue influence will be held to have been committed if the elector having made up his mind to cast a vote for a particular candidate does not do so because 'of the act of the offender, and this can only be if he is under the threat or fear of some adverse consequences. Whenever any threat of adverse consequences is given it will tend to divert the elector from freely exercising his electoral right by voting for the candidate chosen by him for the purpose. In a case where the voter is threatened with an injury as defined in the Indian Penal Code, it has to be deemed under Section 171C (2) (a) that it interferes with the free exercise of the electoral right of the voter and the same applies if the elector is induced or attempt is made to induce him to believe that he or any person in whom he is interested will become or will be rendered an object of divine displeasure or of spiritual censure. There can, however, be cases where the threat may not he of an injury as defined in Section 44 I.P.C., where the harm caused must be illegal.

Mere propaganda against a candidate cannot be held to be exercise of undue influence. The word free is used in Section 171C of I.P.C. as 'qualifying exercise' and not as 'qualifying' the word 'vote'. If undue influence bad been interference with the exercise of free vote, possibly the definition could have been construed as indicating that influence brought on the mind of a voter so as to change the manner of his voting by affecting his choice and judgment in selecting the candidate for whom he is going to cast his vote would be comprised within undue influence. The word free having been used as qualifying the word 'exercise' gives the indication that the freedom envisaged is to cast the vote in accordance with the choice already arrived at and. if such freedom of casting the vote in that manner is interfered with the offence of undue influence it will be held to have been committed.

Section 171G clearly recognizes, that, at elections, there is bound to be propaganda in which candidates or their supporters may be issuing statements so as to influence the voters against their rival candidates, and it limits the prohibition by law to only those statements of fact which are false, or believed to be false, or believed not to be true, in relation to the personal character or conduct of any candidate. These false statements about the personal character and conduct of the candidate may, of course, be scurrilous and foul, but even then, the offence committed would fall under Section 171G I.P.C. which makes the offence punishable with the fine only. On, the other hand, an offence of undue influence as defined in Section 171C I.P.C has been made punishable under Section 171F I.P.C. with imprisonment of either description for a term which may extend to one year or with fine, or with both. If it is held that false propaganda against personal character or conduct of a candidate can amount to undue influence the person indulging in that propaganda would become liable to punishment under Section 171F I.P.C. which has been considered a more serious offence by being made punishable with imprisonment in addition to, or, in the alternative with fine. This interpretation would thus make Section 171G I.P.C. totally ineffective. If the false statements as to personal character or conduct are held to be punishable under Section 171F as constituting the offence of undue influence, there would be no point in prosecuting the same person for the less serious offence under Section 171G.

In the Representation of the People Act, 1951 also, undue influence is defined in almost the same language as that contained in Section. 171C I.P.C. In that Act an election can be declared void not only on the ground of commission of the corrupt practice of undue influence, but also on the ground of publication of false propaganda as to the personal character or conduct of a candidate. Parliament, however, chose not to include any such provision in Act 31 of 1952 which was passed when the Representation of the People Act, 1951 had already been enacted and enforced. The omission may be deliberate or accidental but, in either case, it is not for the court to attempt to fill up this gap by enlarging the meaning to be given to the expression 'undue influence, which is the corrupt practice included in the Act as a ground for setting aside the election, the Supreme Court stated. It is clear from the scheme of Ch. IXA of the Indian Penal Code that false propaganda as to the personal character and conduct of a candidate was created as a separate offence and the definition given in Section 171C of undue influence was not intended to lay down that such propaganda will amount to interference with the free exercise of electoral right so as to constitute undue influence.

In the present case the contents of the pamphlet in question did not contain any threat of a nature, it was stated, which would constitute undue influence as explained above. But even on the assumption that the publication of this pamphlet could constitute undue influence the election of the respondent was not liable to be set aside because it had not been proved that the distribution by post or in the Central Hall of Parliament was with the connivance of the respondent or had materially affected the result of the election. The only difference between the Act of 1951 and the Act of 1952 lies in the fact that under the latter Act corrupt practice of bribery and undue influence by one who was not a party to the election or his agent are also brought in. But the nature and character of undue influence under both the Acts remains the same. There is no reason for taking the view that what would not be undue influence under the Act of 1951 can become one under the Act of 1952.

If publication of any defamatory matter relating to a candidate was to be treated as a direct or indirect interference or an attempt to interference with the exercise of any electoral right-under the wide words of Section 171C(1), there would have been no occasion for the legislature to provide for it separately under Section 123(4) of the Act of 1951. The same position would obtain under the Act of 1952, and before any publication of defamatory matter relating to a candidate can be treated as commission of the offence of undue influence there must be some overt act in addition to the mere publication, some attempt or persuasion of a voter to restrain the free choice of a candidate before,the law of undue influence is excited. The decided cases, it was stated, are sufficient to reject the respondent's contention that in order to establish undue influence it must be shown that there was some threat to a voter or at least an element of compulsion in the appeal to him. The cases also show that it would be futile to attempt to lay down a simple test applicable to all sets of facts and circumstances where undue influence is alleged to have been exercised. It can however be said that an attempt on the part of anybody to deflect a voter will take away from a particular candidate by creating prejudice against or hatred for him, as for instance by casting false aspersions on his personal conduct and character whether by spoken words or in writing may be sufficient for the purpose of establishing the commission of undue influence. Much would however depend on the nature of the attempt, the position of the person making it, and the manner in which it is made. The mere publication by postal dispatch of an anonymous but scurrilous pamphlet relating to the personal character of a candidate to voters all and sundry might attract the operation of Section 171G of the Indian Penal Code but would fall short of Section 171C. But if such a pamphlet is pressed upon voters and methods of inducement applied to them, specially by others who are equally interested in the election, different considerations may well arise. In such a case, a court of law may legitimately hold that the disseminators of the pamphlet were attempting to canalise or force the will of others away from the person whose character was assailed.

2

President vs Prime Minister and Council of Ministers

In his note dated October 6, 1950 on the President's powers, the Attorney-General M.C. Setalvad stated that the Preamble declares that the people of India have resolved to constitute India into a Sovereign Democratic Republic. Article 53 vests the executive powers of the Union in the President. It has to be exercised by him directly or through officers subordinate to him. This Article does not, however, prevent Parliament from conferring by law functions on authorities other than the President. The President has, by virtue of Article 74, in the exercise of his functions is to be aided and advised by the Council of Ministers. By Article 75 the Council of Ministers has been made collectively responsible to the House of the People. This shows the supremacy of the House of the People in the governance of the country. The House of the People, constituted in the manner provided in the Constitution represents the people. The Council of Ministers has to be such which should have the confidence of the House of the People. By the Constitution the President is required to act in all matters with the aid and advice of the Council of Ministers.

Historically, the key provisions of the position of the President in our Constitution appear to be very similar to that of the King in the British Constitution. The President like the King is the formal head of the Executive, all actions of the Union being taken in his name. It must not, however, be overlooked that this executive action derives its force from the Council of Ministers who, in their turn, represent the electorate. In the United Kingdom, the present position of the King in the Constitution has been reached as a result of a long evolutionary process.

By sub-section (2) of Article 53 the Supreme Command of the Defence Forces of the Union vests in the President. This is one of the functions of the President to be exercised by him with the advice of his Council of Ministers. This provision would appear to confer on him no independent power in regard to (a) the appointment, (b) the discipline, (c) the disposition, and (d) the use of the Armed Forces. It would be against the basis of the Constitution that the President should in any of these matters be competent to act independently of or against the advice of his Ministers. The supremacy of the legislature in regard to this matter is implicit in sub-clause (2) of the Article which provides that the exercise of the powers of the supreme command of the Defence Forces by the President shall be regulated by law.

Under Article 123 (a) of the Constitution every judge of the Supreme Court is to be appointed by the President by warrant under his hand and seal after consultation with such judges of the Supreme Court and the States' High Courts as the President may deem necessary. This function of the President would clearly appear to be one of his executive functions to be performed by him with the aid and advice of the Council of Ministers.

The same position holds in regard to the appointment of the Comptroller and Auditor-General. It appears that the President has no independent authority to deal with the Comptroller and Auditor-General. If the President has reasons to believe that 'there is some thing wrong in which the Ministry is concerned' or that 'the Comptroller and Auditor-General has been for some reason or other unable or unwilling to keep a proper check and audit and that the inability, unwillingness or inactivity' suits the Ministry the Parliament is entitled, acting under Article 78, he can call upon the Prime Minister to furnish to him all necessary information in regard to these matters.

The power to appoint the Union Public Service Commission vests with the President. It appears to be one of the functions to be exercised by him with the advice of his Ministers under Article 74. Similar are the functions of the President for the removal and suspension of members under Article 317, the making of regulations as to the conditions of service of members under Article 318, and in the matter of the report of the Commission under Article 323. The President, it seems, has no power to interfere with the exercise of the functions by the Commission apart from the Ministry even if the Commission is acting "unfairly in collusion with the Minister." The President will in such circumstances be entitled to draw the attention of the Prime Minister to the state of affairs and use his position and influence to bring about an improvement.

This is equally applicable to the case of the Election Commission of India. The President, it seems, is not competent to act independently of his Council of Ministers "to ensure free and fair elections" in a case of collusion between the Commission and the Party in power or the Party in opposition. In a democratic system, as in India, the Party in power and the Party in opposition act as a check and counter-check, one against the other.

Article 79 provides that the Parliament for the Union shall consist *inter alia* of the President. It is as a part of Parliament that the assent of the President is necessary under Article 111 to Bills passed by the House of Parliament. This Article provides that a Bill passed by the Houses of Parliament shall be presented to the President whereupon the President shall declare that he assents to the Bill or he withholds assent therefrom. He may also, if the Bill is not a Money Bill, return the Bill to the House with a message asking them to reconsider it or any of its specified provisions. The President is required by the Constitution not to withhold his assent from a Bill duly reconsidered by the House of Parliament and passed again. The President has similar functions under Article 201 in regard to Bills passed by State Legislatures and reserved by a Governor for the consideration of the President.

All these functions have to be exercised by the President in conformity with Article 74 with the advice of his Ministers. If a Bill is passed by the Houses of Parliament and comes for the President's assent he cannot, acting independently of his Council of Ministers, withhold his assent to it, even though he may disapprove it. Such action would create a direct opposition between the elected representatives of the People on the one hand and the President on the other and bring about a deadlock. Even the power to return for reconsideration is to be exercised by him with the advice of the Ministers. It may be that Parliament, in passing legislation, made amendments to it which, in the opinion of the Council of Ministers, go too far or are not in the interest of the country. In such cases, the Council of Ministers would advice the President to withhold assent and return the Bill for reconsideration in the Houses of Parliament. This shows that the President's functions reduce him to the position occupied by the King in the Constitution of the United Kingdom.

Is the President powerless to exercise a certain measure of influence on legislation?. Under Article 78, all the decisions of the Council of Ministers in regard to proposals for legislation will be communicated to him. Even if not so communicated the President will be entitled to have furnished to him by the Prime Minister such information as he needs as regards proposals for legislations. He can also keep himself abreast of developments in regard to Bills under discussion by the Houses of Parliament. He could communicate his views in regard to pending and proposed legislation to his Council of Ministers. If the President happens not to agree with the Council of Ministers on the matter of some proposed legislation he could try and persuade the Ministers to his point of view. If he does not succeed, the supremacy of the House of the People being provided for by the Constitution, he has to accept the advice of the Council of Ministers who are responsible to the House of the People.

Various Articles of the Constitution confer on the President emergency powers. Article 123 which confers on the President the power of the emergency legislation makes the power exercisable if "the President is satisfied that circumstances exist which render it necessary for him to take immediate action." Similarly, Article 352 (1) speaks of the satisfaction of the President "that a grave emergency exists whereby the security of India or any part of the territory thereof is threatened." It seems that despite the condition of the exercise of these powers, the President is obliged to act with the aid and advice of his Ministers. It will be for the Ministry of the day to reach a decision as to whether an emergency of the kind contemplated by the Constitution does or does not exist. In the course of reaching this decision and moving the President to take action pursuant to the decision of the President will, no doubt, have to be persuaded that the emergency does exist. He can, in the course of the discussion, put his point of view to the Council of Ministers and try to influence their action. If he fails to persuade the Council of Ministers and there is a difference of opinion between the President and the Council of Ministers the President will, notwithstanding the difference of views, have to accept the advice of his Ministers.

Article 78 in the case of the President and Article 167 in the case of the Governors provide mechanism by which the President and the Governor have respectively to be furnished information as to the affairs of the Union or the State, as the case may be. The Constitution seems to contemplate the Prime Minister as representing the Council of Ministers being the point of contact between the President on the one hand and the Council of Ministers, on the other. This provision necessarily results in the inference that it would not be open to the President to have direct access to the various departments under the control of each of the Ministers. It may be that in order to ensure the efficient supply of information to the President as contemplated by the Constitution the Prime Minister or the other Ministers may arrange for information to be supplied to the President direct by the Secretaries of the department and may also arrange for the President interviewing those Secretaries from time to time, as he may require. This, however, will not be a matter of the exercise of his rights by the President but rather machinery devised in order to give effect to the requirements of Article 78. No doubt, the position which obtained at the time when Governors used to be appointed by the British and the reasons for the practice of preventing Secretaries having access to the Governors have no application now.

In the United Kingdom, the King has a discretion in selecting the Prime Minister and in dissolving Parliament either at the instance of the Prime Minister or when he feels that there is a patent disharmony between the policy of the Ministry and public opinion. It may be that the Party which came into power at the election may have outgrown its popular hold. Indications of this would appear in opinions expressed in the Press and otherwise. Normally and in accordance with the constitutional practice, the Prime Minister would, in such a case, himself advise the dissolution of Parliament so that could be ascertained whether the Ministry commands the confidence of the people. In dissolving Parliament in such circumstances the King will be really acting on the advice of his Ministers. If the constitutional course mentioned above is not adopted the King may have to dissolve Parliament acting on his own. This, however, would be an exceptional case and very unlikely to arise. The position of the President in India would, in similar circumstances, be analogous to that of the King in the United Kingdom.

Some Conventions and Practices

The President's role as defender of the Constitution and the powers as Head of State, especially in relation to those exercised by the Prime Minister as leader of the government, have changed over time. In particular, presidents have made a number of interventions into government and lawmaking, which have established and challenged some conventions concerning presidential intervention. There have been some important cases.

In 1979, Prime Minister Charan Singh did not enjoy a Parliamentary majority. He responded to this by simply not advising the President to summon Parliament. Since then, presidents have been more diligent in directing incoming prime ministers to convene Parliament and prove their majority within reasonable deadlines (2 to 3 weeks). In the interim period, the prime ministers are generally restrained from making policy decisions.

The Constitution gives the President the power to return a bill unsigned but it circumscribes the power to send it back only once for reconsideration. If the Parliament sends back the bill with or without changes, the President is bound to sign it.

Since the 1990s, Parliamentary elections have generally not resulted in a single party or group of parties having a distinct majority. In such cases, presidents have used their discretion and directed prime ministerial aspirants to establish their credentials before being invited to form the government. Typically, the aspirants have been asked to produce letters from various party leaders, with the signatures of all the MPs who are pledging support to their candidature. This is in addition to the requirement that a Prime Minister proves that he/she has the support of the Lok Sabha (by a vote on the floor of the House) within weeks of being sworn in to office.

Since the Constitution does not provide any time limit within which the President is to declare his assent or refusal, the President could exercise this veto by not taking any action for an indefinite time; but if the ministry has a strong backing in Parliament, it would not be possible for him/her to do so even though he/she can do it. Pocket Veto was used in 1986 by the then President Zail Singh in the Postal Bill.

In the late 1990s, President K.R. Narayanan introduced the important practice of explaining to the nation by means of Rashtrapati Bhavan communiqués the thinking that led to the various decisions he took while exercising his discretionary powers; this has led to openness and transparency in the functioning of the President.

In mid-2006, President A. P. J. Abdul Kalam sent back a controversial bill regarding enlarging the scope of the offices of profit, which would disqualify a person from being a Member of Parliament. The combined opposition, the NDA, hailed the move. The UPA chose to send the bill back to the President without any change and, after 30 days, Kalam gave his assent on August 30, 2006.

3

Procedure for Election

Majority of the members in the Constituent Assembly after a great deal of debate decided in favour of an indirectly elected President. The factors that seems to have influenced their decision were:

a) His little effective powers in the constitutional set up of the country,
b) The large size of the Indian electorate,
c) The financial burden on the exchequer to elect a non-functional head of the state, and
d) Aspirations of an elected President for more powers.

Article 53 of the Indian Constitution lays down that the President shall be elected by an electoral college consisting of

a) The elected members the Indian Constitution and Members of Parliament, and
b) The elected members of the state legislature assemblies. i.e. MLAs. The significance of including Legislative Assemblies in the Electoral College is to ensure a non-partisan election of the President. If only the Parliament elects the President it is just possible that the party having a comfortable majority can get its candidate elected easily. But when the Legislative Assemblies join the Electoral College the position might just be different in view of the party positions in different Assemblies.

Secret Ballot and Parity Between States and Union

The President of India is elected according to secret ballot by the system of proportional representation through single transferable vote. It is through traditional ballot box and not by electronic voting machine (EVM).

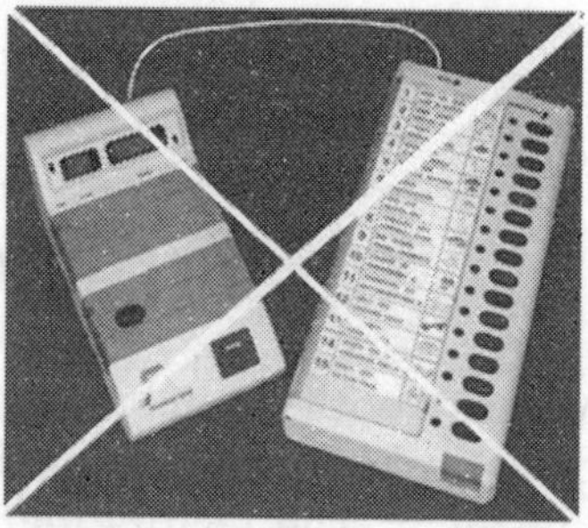

An attempt is made to secure the uniformity of representation of the different states, according to population and the total number of elected members of legislative Assembly of each state so that parity may be maintained between the state as a whole and the union. This has been done to ensure that the votes of the states shall be equal to that of population of the country. This makes the representation of the President broad-based.

In the election of the President the weightage system is used to bring about parity between the votes of the members of Parliament and the members of the Assemblies. Since the strength of legislative assemblies differ owing to differences in population the exact weight of votes of the members of the Assemblies are determined by a definite formula by dividing the population of the concerned state by the total number of elected members of the Assembly which is further divided by one thousand. If the remainder is less than 500 it is should not be taken into account. If it is more than 500 the number should be increased by one.

Proportional Representation

Article 55(3) of the Indian Constitution requires that the President should be elected in accordance with the system of proportional representation by means of the single transferable vote. The underlying principle of proportional representation is to prevent the exclusion of minorities from the benefits of the State, and to give each minority group an effective share in the political life. The aim of proportional representation is to give every division of opinion among electors corresponding to representation in national or local assemblies. In the ordinary mode of election, known as "straight voting system", what happens is that a candidate getting the support of the numerically largest group is elected, although the combined strength of all other candidates representing different other parties may far out-number his supporters. The result is that the elected candidate cannot be said to represent the opinion of the majority of the electorate as a whole. The following illustrations will amply reveal this fact.

In Nandigram South (Midnapore) constituency of the West Bengal State, the following is the ledger of polling:

P.C. Jena (Congress)	15,320
Bhupal Panda (Communist Party)	14,926
I.C. Mahapatra (BJP)	5,204
K.L. Bera (KMPP)	3,184
	38,634

It may be noticed that though 23,314 people voted against the Congress and only 15,320 in favour of it, yet the seat went to the Congress.

This kind of anomaly is sought to be avoided by the system of Proportional Representation, and it is claimed that if this system is practised all the parties or shades of political opinion amongst the electorate will secure the number of seats in the elected body according to their respective strength amongst the electorate.

How the Single Transferable Vote System Works

The best known form of Proportional Representation is that of the "Single Transferable Vote", which means that each elector has only one vote, irrespective of the number of seats to be filled up. For instance, if there are six seats to be filled up, the elector does not cast six votes but indicates six successive preferences, by marking his first preference and the succeeding preferences with the appropriate numerals against the name of candidates printed on his ballot paper.

In the case of the election of the President and the Vice-President there is, however, only one member to be elected. In this case, the Government of India has, nevertheless, prescribed the manner in which the proportional representation is to work. The method prescribed is generally known as the "alternative vote" in a single-member constituency. The following illustration would explain it more fully.

The total number of valid votes is 15,000 and there are four candidates, A,B,C,D. Suppose, they have polled votes as follows:

A 5,250
B 4,800
C 2,700
D 2,250

In the ordinary system of election by simple majority vote, A would be elected forthwith since a voter in this system marks only one preference and as such no question of counting any further preferences, say the second or the third, arises. In the case of the "alternative vote system" it is, however, not so, as it may be that the second best candidate may be declared elected, as against the candidate who might have secured the majority of first preference votes. In the illustration mentioned above the quota will be -

$$\frac{15,000}{1+1}+1=7501$$

No candidate who secures less than 7,501 votes can, in this case of election through the system of proportional representation, be elected. It thus follows that if a candidate is able to secure 7,501 or more first preference votes in his favour, he is immediately declared elected and there does not remain any need to take a second or subsequent count. But if, as in the given case, no candidate has secured this quota, the subsequent preferences have to be counted, until a candidate securing the prescribed limit of votes is found out. The Presidential and Vice-Presidential Election Rules 1952 prescribes the procedure for counting up the subsequent preferences as follows:

If at the end of the first or any subsequent count, the total number of votes credited to any candidate is equal to, or greater than, the quota, or there is any one continuing candidate, that candidate is declared elected.

If at the end of any count, no candidate can be declared elected -

(a) exclude the candidate who up to that stage has been credited with the lowest number of votes;

(b) examine all the ballot papers in his parcel and sub-parcels, arrange the unexhausted papers in sub-parcels according to the next available preferences recorded thereon for the continuing candidates; count the number of votes in each such sub-parcel and credit it to the candidate for whom such preference is recorded; transfer the sub-parcel of all the exhausted papers; and

(c) see whether any of the continuing candidates has, after such transfer and credit, secured the quota. If, when a candidate has to be excluded under clause (a) above, two or more candidates have been credited with the same number of votes and stand lowest on the poll, exclude that candidate who has secured the lowest number of first preferences votes, and if that number also was the same in the case of two or more candidates, decide by lot which of them shall be excluded.

All sub-parcels of exhausted papers referred to in clause (b) above, shall be set apart as finally dealt with and the votes recorded thereon shall not thereafter be taken into account.

It would, therefore, be seen that in case where no member has obtained the quota votes fixed for election, the prescribed method of transfer of votes follows a process of elimination of the candidate who is at the lowest rung in the order of polling according to the first preference and so on, till at last such a candidate is found who has obtained the quota of votes or if there is no such candidate, all candidates except one are, one after the other, eliminated from the field. The candidate who survives the process of elimination is, in such a case, returned as the President or Vice-President, as the case may be.

An application of this process to the illustration given above would reveal that D will be the first to be eliminated, and the second preferences recorded in the 2,250 ballot papers on which he has obtained the first preference will be transferred to the remaining candidates, namely A, B, and C. Supposing in these 2,250 ballot papers the second preferences are recorded as follows:

In favour of

A 300
B 1050
C 900

These will be transferred and added to the first preferences in favour of A, B and C as follows:-

A ..... 5,250 + 300 = 5,550
B ..... 4,800 + 1050 = 5,850
C ..... 2,700 + 900 = 3,600

Now, in the second count, therefore, C having obtained the last number of votes is eliminated and 3,600 votes secured by him are once again transferred to A and B in the order of third preferences recorded thereon. Suppose the third preferences on the 3,600 ballot papers recorded in favour of A and B are 1700 and 1900 respectively the result of this second transfer would then be as under:

A ..... 5,550 + 1,700 = 7,250
B ..... 5,850 + 1,900 = 7,750

B having, therefore, in this case secured the quota of votes is elected and it is no longer necessary to count the fourth preference. The illustration thus shows that although B had secured lesser number of first preferences votes as compared to A, yet B is elected by virtue of the second preferences obtained by him. This apparently anomalous result is justified on the reasoning that if the views of the electors are assessed through the doctrine of proportional representation it is clearly revealed that B is preferred and supported by a numerically larger number of electors than A and as such he is the one elected by a majority.

The present system of election for the President has been adopted under the Constitution of India in order to maintain the neutrality of the head of State, which both the ceremonial functions in any federation and the specific powers under a parliamentary system demand and also to render it acceptable to as wide a body of opinion as possible. But it should be remembered that the presidential office can be kept above political turmoil only if the majority party at the Centre willingly consults minority parties also before a nomination is announced. This is desirable because, despite the provision that for the election of the President the votes of the Members of Parliament be equal to those of the Assemblies of all the States taken together, the possibility cannot be set aside that State Legislatures may, at any time, be dominated by parties other than the party in power at the Centre and in such a case they might be able to defeat a nominee of the majority party at the Centre.

How Voting works out?

(i) "The population of Andhra Pradesh is 43,502,708. Let us take the total number of elected members in the Legislative Assembly of Andhra Pradesh to be 294. To obtain the number of votes which each such elected member will be entitled to cast at the election of the President we have first to divide 43,502,708 (which is the population) by 294 (which is the total number of elected members), and then to divide the quotient by 1,000. In this case, the quotient is 147,968.3945. The number of votes which each such member will be entitled to cast would be 147,968.3945/1000, i.e. 148.

(ii) Again, the population of Punjab is 1,35,51,060. Let us take the total number of elected members of the Legislature of Punjab to be 117. Now, applying the aforesaid process, if we divide 1,35,51,060 (i.e. the population) by 117 (i.e. the total number of elected members), the quotient is 115821.0256. Therefore, the number of votes which each member of Punjab

Legislature would be entitled to cast is 115,821.0256/ 1000 i.e. 116.

Each elected member of either House of Parliament shall have such number of votes as may be obtained by dividing the total number of votes assigned to the members of the Legislative Assemblies of the States under sub-clauses (a) and (b) by the total number of the elected members of both Houses of Parliament, fractions exceeding one-half being counted as one and other fractions being disregarded.

Quota of Votes

There are several ways of finding out the quota, but the most common method is to divide the total number of valid votes cast by the total number of seats in the constituency plus one and add one to the quotient. The formula may be represented as follows:

$$\text{Quota} = \frac{\text{Total number of valid votes cast}}{\text{Total number of seats to be filled} + 1} + 1$$

Suppose, there are 100 valid voting papers and four seats are to be filled up. In order, therefore, to determine the quota 100 is divided by 4 plus 1, i.e. 5 and the quotient arrived at, namely 20, is increased by one so that the quota is 21. After the quota is fixed, any candidate whose total number of first preference votes is equal to or exceeds the quota is forthwith declared elected.

Time Limit for Election

Whenever the presidential office falls vacant on account of his death, resignation or impeachment the Vice-President succeeds him for a period of six months. The election of the President must be conducted within six months from the date of vacancy. In case of resignation, the President hands over the letter to the Vice-President of India.

The Presidential election must be held before the expiration of his term of office. The Election Commission shall issue the notification on or as soon as convenient, may be, after the sixtieth day before the expiration of the term of office of the outgoing President or Vice-President, as the case may be. The election of the President must be completed within the time fixed by Article 62(1). Thus, the time limit is mandatory.

Distribution of Surplus Votes

Each successful candidate's surplus votes of first preferences which are now of no use to him, are transferred to other candidates proportionately to the second preferences indicated on the whole of his papers (except that the second preferences shown for any other candidate already elected are ignored and the third preferences on those papers taken instead). The point is that every vote shall be made effective and not allowed to go waste, while under the ordinary system of representation, the votes of many electors are of no use.

Elimination of the Bottom Candidate

If all the seats are filled upon this second count, the election is completed. But if all the required number of candidates do not reach the quota by the distribution of surplus first preferences votes of the candidates who have received more than the quota, the process is reversed by dropping out the candidate who has the least number of first preferences. The whole of his votes are transferred to the other not yet elected candidates in accordance with the next available preferences shown on his papers (next available means next excluding candidates already elected). If this does not suffice to fill the remaining seat or seats, the process is repeated by the exclusion of the candidate now at the bottom of polls and the transfer of his votes as a whole in accordance with the next available preferences shown on his papers. Eventually, in this way, all seats are filled.

Irrespective of the fact that a number of seats may have to be filled, this system postulates one vote for each voter with the reservation that this single vote is transferred to other candidates. This is the reason why this system is known as "single transferable vote system."

4

Election Petition

It is unfortunate that some candidates have been unsuccessfully contesting elections without having any solid background. Knowing it well that they would not win their purpose had just been to come to limelight. Some of these candidates have even been filing election petitions without any substance and have lost the case. On July 6, 1993, in Petition No.3 of 1992, Chaman Lal Sahu, a lawyer challenged APJ Abdul Kalam's election and the Supreme Court observed that he did so "in a cavalier and light-hearted manner" and hence imposed a fine of Rs.50,000 on Sahu. A five-judge Constitution Bench, headed by Chief Justice G.B. Pattnaik said that Sahu had filed the writ petition and an appeal against the Delhi High Court which had imposed a cost of Rs.20,000 on him. Before this, Sahu had also filed petitions against the elected presidents.

Kaka Joginder Singh, a textile mill owner earned the epithet of *Dharti Pakad*, one who clings to the ground for contesting frequent elections and he was always unsuccessful. He not only contested against leaders like L.K. Advani and Atal Bihari Vajpayee in parliamentary elections but also in presidential election against Shankar Dayal Sharma. He tried elections from 14 states of India in 1990s, mostly of state assemblies. He earned 451 votes (0.23%) in the Ludhiana poll for 1982, 1848 votes (0.88%) again in the Ludhiana poll in 1985, 46 votes in the 1991 New Delhi election, was fourth in the polling for the Nandyal Lok Sabha election of 1991 with 1506 votes (.001%), fourth in the polling for president in 1991, eighth in the polling for the Lucknow Lok Sabha election of 1998 with 212 votes (0.02%). He died on December 23, 1998.

According to Article 71 of the Constitution of India, all doubts and disputes arising out of or in connection with the election of a President or Vice-President shall be enquired into and decided by the Supreme Court only. Further, as per

Section 14 of the Presidential and Vice-Presidential Elections Act, 1952, an election petition can be filed before the Supreme Court. For the sake of clarity it should be worthwhile giving below the relevant excerpts of two Supreme Court cases which indicate the issues involved.

In *Charan Lal Sahu & Others vs Giani Zail Singh & Another 1984* AIR 304, 1984 SCR (2) 6, the question was raised about the maintainability of petitions. It was contended that neither of the two petitioners was a 'candidate' within the meaning of section 13(a) of the Presidential and Vice-Presidential Elections Act, 1952 and since under Section 14A, an election petition can be filed only by a person who was a candidate at the election, the petitioners had no standing to file the petitions. In this case, the Returning Officer accepted the nomination papers of two candidates only, viz. Giani Zail Singh and Justice H.R. Khanna. The election was held on July 12, 1982, and Giani Zail Singh was declared as the successful candidate. The petitioners, who had filed their nomination papers, contested the election on various grounds and alleged that Giani Zail Singh exercised undue influence over the voters through his confidants.

The second case worth mentioning is *Kirpal Singh* vs *V.V. Giri,* 1970 AIR 2097, 1971 SCR (2) 197. Four election petitions filed under Section 14 of the Presidential and Vice-Presidential Election Act (XXXI of 1952) and Article 71 of the Constitution of India challenged the election of V. V. Giri to the office of the President of India. The petitioner Shiv Kirpal Singh was a candidate in the election and so was the other person. The nominations of both these petitioners were rejected by the Returning Officer.

The main question that came up for consideration was whether the distribution of an anonymous pamphlet making defamatory statements about one of the candidates at the election, in the manner alleged by the petitioners, amounted to exercise of undue influence within the meaning of Section 18 of the Presidential and Vice-Presidential Election Act 31 of 1952 read with Section 171 C of the Indian Penal Code. Though the fact who got the pamphlet published and distributed could not be established it was held that the argument completely disregards the structure and provisions of Section 171C. The Section is enacted in three parts. The first stage contains the definition of undue influence. This is in wide terms and renders a person voluntarily interfering or attempting to interfere with the free exercise of any electoral right guilty of committing undue influence. That this is very wide is indicated by the opening sentence of sub-section (2) that is, "without prejudice to the generality of the provisions of sub-section (1)". It is well settled that when the expression is used anything contained in the provisions following this expression is not intended to cut down the generality of the meaning of the preceding provision. It proceeds on the assumption that a declaration of public policy or a promise of public action or the mere exercise of a legal right can interfere with an electoral right, and therefore it provides that if there is no intention to interfere with the electoral right it shall not be deemed to be interference within the meaning of this Section. Such a declaration of public policy or the promise of public action can only act and tend to interfere at the stage when a voter is trying to make up his mind as to which candidate he would support.

The expression "free exercise of the electoral right" does not mean that a voter is not to be influenced. This expression has to be read in the context of an election in a democratic society and the candidates and their supporters must naturally be allowed to canvass support by all legal and legitimate means. This exercise of the right by a candidate or his supporters to canvass support does not interfere or attempt to interfere with the free exercise of the electoral right. What does however attempt to interfere with the exercise of an electoral right is "tyranny over the mind". If the contention of the respondent was to be accepted it would be quite legitimate on the part of the candidate or his supporters to hypnotise a voter and then send him to vote. At the stage of casting his ballot paper there would be no pressure cast on him because his mind has already been made up for him by the hypnotiser.

On the evidence in the case it must be held that the pamphlet in question was distributed by post and in the Central Hall of

Parliament by some members of Parliament and there was wide discussion about it in the Central Hall. The allegations in the pamphlet, made against one of the losing candidates, were covered under Section 171C I.P.C. The argument that the pamphlet could not come under Section 171C because it was anonymously distributed was fallacious. A series of anonymous attempts in a country like ours would have as much, if not more, effect as one open powerful attempt. It would be dangerous to provide a sanctuary for anonymous attempts. Moreover, when Members of Parliament distribute a pamphlet in the Central Hall it has the same effect as if they had endorsed the pamphlet in writing.

Accordingly, it must be held that the distribution of the pamphlet by post as also distribution in the Central Hall constituted an attempt to interfere with the free exercise of the right of vote within Section 18 of the Act. There was however no evidence to show that the respondent had any connection with the pamphlet or with its distribution. Nor was there any evidence to show that anyone connected with the distribution either through the post or in the Central Hall had any contact with the respondent, or that he distributed it with his knowledge or connivance.

It is well settled that the burden of proving that the result of the election has been materially affected is on the petitioners. As held by this Court in *Samant N. Balkrishna* vs *George Fernandes*, the matter cannot be decided on possibility or reasonable judicial guess. On the evidence in the present case it was difficult to hold that the petitioners had proved that the publication and distribution of the pamphlet materially affected the result of the election. It only leads to the conclusion that it probably did have some effect but the vast majority of the electors were able to throw off the effect of the pamphlet and vote according to their own personal wish or according to the mandate of their party.

Justice Bhargava held that sub-section (1) of Section 171C in general terms makes any act an 'undue influence' if it interferes or attempts to interfere with the free exercises of any electoral right and if it is committed voluntarily. The electoral right, according to the definition in Section 171A(b) is the right of a voter to vote or refrain from voting. Undue influence can be held to be committed if the person charged with the offence interferes or attempts to interfere with the free exercise of this right of voting or refraining from voting. When an elector exercises the right of voting it can be envisaged that he goes through the mental process of first taking a decision that he will vote in favour of a particular candidate and thereafter, having made up his mind, he has to go and exercise that electoral right by casting the vote in favour of the candidate chosen by him. The language used in Section 171C indicates that the offence of undue influence comes in at the second stage when the offender interferes or attempts to interfere with the free exercise of that choice of voting in accordance with the decision already taken by the voter. It, therefore, follows that if any acts are done which merely influence the voter in making his choice between one candidate or another, they will not amount to interference with the free exercise of the electoral right. In fact, all canvassing that is carried on and which is considered legitimate is intended to influence the choice of a voter at the first stage and that is quite permissible. Once the choice has been made by the voter, there should be no interference with the free exercise by him of that choice by actually casting the vote, or in the alternative there may be cases where a voter may decide that he will not vote for any candidate at all but some acts are done which compel him to cast his vote. It is in such cases that the offence of undue influence will be held to have been committed.

The language used in the definition of undue influence implies that an offence of undue influence will be held to have been committed if the elector having made up his mind to cast a vote for a particular candidate does not do so because 'of the act of the offender, and this can only be if he is under the threat or fear of some adverse consequence. Whenever any threat of adverse consequences is given it will tend to divert the elector from freely exercising his electoral right by voting for the candidate chosen by him for the purpose. In a case where the voter is threatened with an injury as defined in the Indian Penal Code, it has to be deemed under Section 171C (2) (a) that it interferes with the free exercise of the electoral right of the voter and the same applies if the elector is induced or attempt is made to induce him to believe that he or any person in whom he is interested will become or will be rendered an object of divine displeasure or of spiritual censure. There can, however, be cases where the threat may not be of an injury as defined in Section 44 I.P.C., where the harm caused must be illegal.

Mere propaganda against a candidate cannot be held to be exercise of undue influence. The word free is used in Section 171C I.P.C. as 'qualifying exercise' and not as 'qualifying' the word 'vote'. If undue influence bad been interference with the exercise of free vote, possibly the definition could have been construed as indicating that influence brought on the mind of a voter so as to change the manner of his voting by affecting his choice and judgment in selecting the candidate for whom he is going to cast his vote would be comprised within undue influence. The word free having been used as qualifying the word 'exercise' gives the indication that the freedom envisaged is to cast the vote in accordance with the choice already arrived at and. if such freedom of casting the vote in that manner is interfered with the offence of undue influence it will be held to have been committed.

Section 171G clearly recognizes that, at elections, there is bound to be propaganda in which candidates or their supporters may be issuing statements so as to influence the voters against their rival candidates, and it limits the prohibition by law to only those statements of fact which are false, or believed to be false, or believed not to be true, in relation to the personal character or conduct of any candidate. These false statements about the personal character and conduct of the candidate may, of course, be scurrilous and foul, but even then, the offence committed would fall under Section 171G I.P.C. which makes the offence punishable with the fine only. On, the other hand, an offence of undue influence as defined in Section 171C I.P.C has been made punishable under Section 171F I.P.C. with imprisonment of either description for a term which may extend to one year or with fine, or with both. If it is held that false propaganda against personal character or conduct of a candidate can amount to undue influence the person indulging in that propaganda would become liable to punishment under Section 171F I.P.C. which has been considered a more serious offence by being made punishable with imprisonment in addition to, or, in the alternative with fine. This interpretation would thus make Section 171G I.P.C. totally ineffective. If the false statements as to personal character or conduct are held to be punishable under Section. 171F as constituting the offence of undue influence, there would be no point in prosecuting the same person for the less serious offence under Section 171G.

If publication of any defamatory matter relating to a candidate was to be treated as a direct or indirect interference or an attempt to interference with the exercise of any electoral right-under the wide words of Section 171C(1), there would have been no occasion for the legislature to provide for it separately under Section 123(4) of the Act of 1951, it was observed. The same position would obtain under the Act of 1952, and before any publication of defamatory matter relating to a candidate can be treated as commission of the offence of undue influence there must be some overt act in addition to the mere publication, some attempt or persuasion of a voter to restrain the free choice of a candidate before the law of undue influence is excited.

Part II

Sucessive Presidents

5

Rajendra Prasad

Tenure as President
26 Jan 1950-13 May 1962
Votes Secured: 507,400
Nearest Rival
K.T. Shah
Votes Secured: 92,827

1884-1963

"In Dr Rajendra Prasad we have one who embodies the spirit of gentleness and the gospel of India. He is the soul of goodness; he has great patience and courage...He is the suffering servant of India", said Dr Radhakrishnan in a tribute to Dr Rajendra Prasad on the latter's election as President of the Constituent Assembly. Aptly called 'the gentleman of Indian politics', Dr Rajendra Prasad, the first President of the Republic of India, who presided over India's Constituent Assembly for the drafting of Indian Constitution, was a great jurist, a scholar and an embodiment of Hindu ideal of 'simple living and high thinking'. He was urbane and courteous as a President and maintained the independence, dignity and prestige of the high office. Having been involved in the freedom struggle, contact with the masses both as a freedom fighter and as Minister for Food and Agriculture in the Interim Ministry before the country's Independence, with his deep religious faith and humble beginning he endeared himself to everyone with his dignity, humility and vast knowledge of national affairs and the Constitution.

Born in a small house located in Zeradei village in the State of Bihar, on December 3, 1884, Rajendra Prasad was the son of Munshi Madvadev Sahai who was himself a scholar of Persian and Sanskrit and was fond of wrestling, horticulture and gave Ayurvedic and Unani treatment to the patients who flocked to him. His mother was a devout lady who brought up Rajendra to cherish the best ideals of ancient culture and traditions. She narrated to him the stories from *The Ramayana* and sang devotional songs to lull him to sleep. All this left an indelible impact on Rajendra Prasad. Love of the country and devotion to Dharma took early roots in him and obviously his parents had a great influence in moulding his character.

Since there was no school in the village Zeradei, a *maulvi* (Muslim teacher) was engaged to teach Rajendra and his two cousins Persian and Urdu at a remuneration of four rupees. The *Maktab* (school) was located in a *verandah* of Maulvi Saheb's house where the pupils were required to sit on a *takhatposh* (wooden cot). Rajendra Prasad had to study in the light of an oil lamp. The first education Rajendra had was in the name of *Allah*. Maulvi Saheb taught them the alphabet by covering a bit of plastered raised ground with coal dust, and the pupils had to practice writing the alphabet and the figures on this with their fingers or chalk. After completing his primary education, he was admitted in a school in Chapra, twenty-three miles away, to learn English—the language of the rulers. His studious nature and quick grasp earned him a double promotion in the very first year, and he soon topped his examinations. In 1902, he secured first rank in the matriculation examination of the Calcutta University.

At the age of 14, Rajendra Prasad was married to Rajbansi Devi. The early marriage was enjoined by ancient custom. Young Rajendra was hardly in a position to resist this move, particularly having been brought up in an atmosphere of filial obedience and conformity with traditions. Like the game of dolls, which he used to play with his sister, people in his marriage procession carried him to the bridegroom's house in a *palanquin*. The bride was brought to the husband's house after a year and became the responsibility of the family and Rajendra was left free to pursue his studies. For years, they saw little of each other and the first child was born after ten years. The young bride had to veil her face not only in the presence of males but even before her mother-in-law. It was considered bad for everyone to visit his wife's room during the day time so much so that in later years, when his wife had an attack of cholera, young Rajendra was not permitted to see her. In spite of all this, women in the household exercised great influence over the men and built up an ambience of dignity and affection which enabled them to share the joys and sorrows of their husbands, sons and brothers and ensured well-knit families.

After matriculation, Rajendra was admitted in the Presidency College at Calcutta (now, Kolkatta). Though the massive buildings, wide roads and rumbling tram-cars thrilled Rajendra, the malarial attacks, strain of work and sometimes changes in the climate brought him violent attacks of asthma. In his college, he was greatly attracted to science but could not master mathematics. At the university, he had a brilliant career, coming first in every examination for the Bachelor's degree and winning several scholarships. Books did not occupy all his time and he mixed freely with everybody and became a social figure. Because of his simple straight-forward nature and unassuming manners, he was elected Secretary of the College Union.

The new consciousness aroused in Bengal by persons like Raja Ram Mohun Roy, Swami Vivekananda and Rabindranath Tagore made a deep impact on him. The social reforms sponsored by Raja Ram Mohun Roy, Keshab Chander Sen and others broke the power of orthodoxy, which had for long oppressed men and women and kept them ignorant and backward. On the political front, a storm had arisen over the partition of Bengal in 1905. The writings of B. Dutt and Aurobindo Ghosh had stirred the conscience of the people. In search of a weapon to fight the British the country took to *swadeshi*, i.e. boycotting all articles of foreign manufacture. In Bengal, the movement spread like a wildfire. Rajendra Prasad pondered deeply over the prevailing events, both social and political. He was gradually drawn to the constructive field of work. He became a member of the Dawn Society which aimed at widening the horizon of the students and building up their character. Attendance of its regular classes and lectures instilled in him the habit of social work. He organized all the Bihari students in Calcutta and brought them in the Bihari Club. In 1906, he organized the Bihari Students Conference.

After taking his M.A in 1908, Rajendra Prasad took up the post of a professor in Muzaffarpur College. But the profession did not appeal to him and his brother advised him to pursue legal studies. When he was steadily building up a legal career in 1910, he came in contact with Gopal Krishna Gokhale, and, as advised by the latter, wanted to join the Servants of India Society with a view to serve the country. But the family resisted and he had to give up the idea. He returned to Calcutta to continue his legal studies and started his training under Khan Bahadur, an eminent lawyer and leader of Muslims. In 1911, he started his legal practice and his integrity, hard work and sound knowledge of law drew more and more clients to him. Sir Ashutosh Mukherji, Judge of the High Court, was so impressed with his masterly presentation of law that, as Vice Chancellor of the University, he offered him the post of Professor of Law. The judges placed great reliance on his arguments because they felt that they were based on a deep study of law and conscientious presentation of the case. As an advocate, he never accepted a case which could not be argued properly. He preferred to tell such a client that there was nothing to be gained by filing a suit.

In 1915, after obtaining the degree of Master of Law in the first division, Rajendra Prasad shifted his practice to Patna. In Bihar, he was ranked among the leading advocates and had a flourishing and lucrative practice. He started taking greater interest in political activity and was drawn to the Indian National Congress. Tilak, who had endeavoured to give the Congress an aggressive outlook, was still in jail and the field was free for the moderates. The English-speaking upper middle classes dominated the Congress. When the World War broke in 1914, the moderates became disenchanted with the Allies. Gopal Krishna Gokhale's death in February 1915 left the field to Tilak who, in his commentary on the *Gita*, written in prison, preached courageous action with no desire for the fruit thereof. The book had a tremendous effect in vitalizing political and social life of Rajendra Prasad. At Congress session in 1915, he came in contact with Mahatma Gandhi who had just brought with him a great reputation for his unique achievement in South Africa, and whose struggle marked a turning point in the life of Rajendra Prasad. When the World War neared its end, Rajendra Prasad felt that political activity had gathered much momentum due to economic discontent. The price spiral of food grains, oils, cloth and other household articles was mounting. The famous slogan of Bal Gangadhar Tilak in April 1916 stirred the country and wielded great influence in the Congress. A number of activities and events aroused deep indignation in him and strengthened his determination to fight for the freedom of the country. He felt that he must play an active part in the freedom movement and took up editing a new Hindi weekly called *Desh*. He also worked in the editorial board of *Searchlight*, English bi-weekly.

In 1932, Rajendra Prasad was elected President of the Congress session to be held in Orissa. He was called upon to preside over the Congress session in 1934 in Bombay (now: Mumbai). He was given a rousing reception by the people, thus indicating their support of the Congress and their confidence in him. He conducted the proceedings with firmness and impartiality. He also did a whirlwind tour of many provinces and devoted himself in revitalizing the Congress organization which had grown limp and listless for some time. He was the first President of the Congress organization to tour throughout the country addressing the workers, getting into personal contact with them and giving the guidance and encouragement. During his tenure, he made a single handed attempt to reach an agreement with Jinnah to modify the communal award.

As President of the Nagpur session of the Hindi Sahitya Sammelan in 1935, Rajendra Prasad reiterated his faith in one language for the whole country which can be Hindi. It should be simple Hindi, he said, which should adopt words from all Indian languages and dialects.

In the Interim Ministry, which was formed on September 2, 1946, Rajendra Prasad was allotted the portfolio of Food and Agriculture. It was at a time when there was not enough food in the country for the growing population. Born and bred on the soil, he was closest to the farmers and understood their difficulties and their aspirations. In view of the overall shortage, the Government sought the cooperation of the provincial and the major state governments and made arrangements for the surpluses to be placed at the disposal of the Central Government to be sent to the deficit areas with a view to have an equitable distribution throughout the country. A basic plan of procurement and distribution of food grains was formulated at the end of each crop season. This had to be adjusted every month from the surplus areas to give to the common pool the maximum quantity that they could get from the farmers, and to distribute whatever was available to the deficit areas, supplementing it with imports from abroad. Dr Rajendra Prasad appealed to the producers to grow more food and to the consumers to use food wisely and not to waste it. He surveyed the situation carefully and felt that the long-term solution of the food problem lay in increasing production by revitalizing agriculture, which had suffered from serious neglect for centuries. The yields from land had declined and were about the lowest in the world. Production on 82 per cent of the land depended entirely on the vagaries of the weather. He felt that it was going to be an uphill task to repair this damage to agriculture. Therefore, he decided that the farmers should be helped by the grant of substantial subsidies to dig wells and use better seed, fertilizers and implements. He got the Cabinet to sanction larger grants for this purpose.

Rajendra Prasad also initiated measures for fixing maximum prices of food grains in parity with the price level of the main commodities. The provincial governments were pressed to revise their land tenure laws, abolishing intermediaries. The tenants were provided the fixity of tenure at reasonable rent with the option to purchase the landlords' rights at a reasonable price. Having been himself brought up on the land, he felt that the cow was not only a useful animal but "a mother of prosperity." A good bull was essential to agriculture. He urged the proper care of cattle as an economic necessity. He advocated the scientific management of *goshalas* (cattle homes). But his tenure as Food Minister was too short to bring in substantial improvements. Dr Rajendra Prasad had to resign as Food Minister to take over the helm of the Congress as its President for the third time.

As President of the Congress, Dr Rajendra Prasad played an important role in Mahatma Gandhi's last fast. The news of the fast spread consternation throughout the country. At the age of 78, Mahatma Gandhi was playing with death by undergoing this fast. Urgent and immediate action was necessary to save his life. Dr Rajendra Prasad had protracted discussions with various leaders and ultimately a joint declaration was issued stating that it was the heartfelt desire of Hindus, Muslims and Sikhs and all other communities to live in Delhi like brothers, and that they pledged their lives, property and faith for the restoration of conditions for peaceful co-existence. Mahatma Gandhi was satisfied that a change of heart had occurred and broke the fast.

When the Constituent Assembly was convened on December 9, 1946, with a view to draft the Constitution for India, Dr Rajendra Prasad became its President. The Assembly met in an atmosphere of tension owing to the intransigence of the Muslim League, which had not only boycotted the Constituent Assembly but had initiated 'direct action' in the country, leading to bloodshed and carnage on a an unprecedented scale. It was imperative that the work of the Assembly should be carried on in such a way as to lesson the feeling of distrust and hostility of Muslims. As President of the Assembly he maintained a neutral attitude and his firmness in handling the proceedings won him the admiration of the people. His impartiality inspired confidence among the members of the minorities and those who differed from the Congress. However, his most valuable contribution was behind the scenes. There were internal contradictions, not only among the various communities represented in the Assembly but even within the Congress Party. Some were bent on having a strong Union Government while others attached great values to the Fundamental Rights of the people. Those conflicting views were held even by top leaders and as President he secured impartial and unfettered discussion. His deep erudition and sound knowledge of jurisprudence were freely available to all members, who frequently sought his advice on the problems and valued it, for it arose out of a profound study and wide experience of human affairs. With all such qualities, he was unanimously elected as the President of the Indian Republic.

Dr Rajendra Prasad's nomination as the first President of India was hailed with delight by the Indian people. With his unimpeachable personal integrity he could be fully trusted as the custodian of the Constitution. The election took place on April 7, 1952. Dr Rajendra Prasad received 2,896 votes out of a total of 3,486 votes cast and he was sworn in on May 13, 1952. In his broadcast to the nation he said: "My request to all the people of this country is to treat me as one of them and give me the opportunity and encouragement to serve them to the best of my capacity."

Following Independence for India, the postcolonial government led by Jawaharlal Nehru completed the codification and reform of Hindu Personal law, a process that had begun by the British. According to the British policy of non-interference, reform of personal law should have arisen from a demand from the Hindu community. This was not the case, as there was significant opposition from various Hindu politicians, organizations, and devotees who saw themselves unjustly singled out as the sole religious community whose laws were to be reformed. However, the administration saw such codification as necessary in order to unify the Hindu community, which ideally would be a first step towards unifying the nation. They succeeded in passing four Hindu Code Bills: the Hindu Marriage Act (1955), Hindu Succession Act (1956), Hindu Minority and Guardianship Act (1956), and Hindu Adoptions and Maintenance Act (1956).

As President, though Dr Rajendra Prasad worked closely with the then Prime Minister Jawaharlal Nehru, they had differences of opinion on some matters, on the inclusion of the introduction of Hindu Code Bills. Nehru's idealism, his dynamic outlook on life and his deep perception of the forces in the world cast a glamour on Dr Rajendra Prasad. Both were equally revered as representing India in transition from old to the new order of things. The President tried to avoid a crisis of any sort and reached an understanding and never tried to force any issue. But whenever he was inclined to be firm, he was able to convince Nehru of his viewpoint. The postponement for consideration of the Hindu Code Bill in 1951 was one such instance. Public opinion was strongly against rushing this legislation and held that a legislature elected by the indirect vote for the purpose of framing the Constitution was not competent to deal with a matter which affected the traditional roots of Hindu society with regard to marriage and inheritance. It argued that in a country like England the constitutional convention would require that such basic legislation should be undertaken after obtaining a clear verdict of the electorate. If the Prime Minister had pushed the Bill at the tail-end of the session, an embarrassing position would have been created. The President advised the Prime Minister to postpone the Hindu Code Bill. He was prepared to appeal to the legislature by sending a message with the recommendation. Good counsels, however, prevailed and the Government bowed to the force of public opinion and decided to postpone the Bill till the elections were over.

In 1957, when his first tenure was expiring, there was a move to nominate Dr S Radhakrishnan to succeed Dr Rajendra Prasad. But the Parliamentary Board unanimously decided Dr Rajendra Prasad to continue. His personal relations with the then Prime Minister held them together. They, of course, had some differences. "But the differences were not so much on the Congress programmes or procedure in our attitudes", he once said. Their common objective also held them together. Both had confidence and the trust of the people. Dr Rajendra Prasad appealed to the people because of his traditional Indian outlook, his religious approach to life—untrammeled by orthodoxy or bigotry—and his habit of finding the middle way. Nehru's idealism, his dynamic outlook on life and his deep perception of the forces operating in the world cast a glamour around him. The people revered both of them as representing India in transition from the old to the new order of things.

As a staunch vegetarian, Dr Rajendra Prasad's food was the same as that of the common man in India. He believed that a meat diet coarsens the mind and raises thoughts of *himsa*. He never consumed liquor and disliked tobacco. Except on state occasions he always wore home-spun cloth. Being frugal by nature, he reduced his wants to the point of austerity. When he assumed office as President he felt that the salary fixed by the Constitution at Rs.10,000 a month, with a sumptuary allowance of Rs.2,500, was too high. He imposed a series of voluntary cut and reduced it to half of what was provided under the Constitution. He did not draw the sumptuary allowance and entertained his guests out of his own salary. He was freely available to all who desired to meet him. Once he stopped a stately Presidential cavalcade in Delhi to exchange greetings with a peasant in the crowd who had hailed him as "Rajen Babu". During his visits to the holy places he bathed in rivers like a common man on the ground with the people and shared their food with them.

As President, Dr Rajendra Prasad visited a number of countries and advised the Indians residing there to consider themselves as citizens of that country. "But do not forget India. Conduct yourself in a manner so as to enhance the name and prestige of India...You are like the ambassadors of India and you must show the culture and the civilization of your motherland", he counseled them. His visits abroad led to better understanding of India, for he combined the old and the new in India.

During his tenure, Rashtrapati Bhavan had undergone a great change. The old icy, rigid and formal atmosphere of Viceregal Lodge gave way to a cordial and homely atmosphere. Everybody was willing to help. It was a fine sight to see one of the stately red-coated bodyguard helping an old woman who wanted to greet the President personally on his birthday. One part of Rashtrapati Bhavan was handed over for the Cabinet offices. The Central portion was converted into a National Museum, housing ancient treasures of art. The President and his family occupied only one wing of the stately edifice of 340 rooms. He himself had a small suite of two rooms, with a personal temple attached. The exquisite

Moghul Garden was thrown open to the people for one month, every year, during the flowering season. A completely Indian atmosphere was created.

The President personally attended to all mercy petitions for commutation of sentences. His legal training and his keen sense of justice made him to go through the judgments of the courts quite carefully, howsoever voluminous they might be. The upliftment of the *Harijans* (untouchables) was nearer to his heart. He worked for the removal of untouchability and for their economic betterment. He urged them to be clean in their living, acquire education and should not nurse any inferiority complex. He reminded them that 'Constitution can only be what its people want it to be. If you make good use of the Constitutional provisions you will find that they are good enough for you'. He was keenly interested in the tribal welfare. He felt that the problem of unemployment could not be solved entirely through industrialization and that the solution lay in the popularization and improvement of cottage industries. He extended the patronage of Rashtrapati Bhavan to Kashmir carpets and silviculture and also to Manipur embroidery. He was a great advocate of the basic system of education.

The President's views on some of the burning problems of the day are usually contained in his secret letters to the Prime Minister. In one of his letters he referred to co-operative farms, redistribution of agricultural holdings and state trading in food grains. He also referred to the Prime Minister about the allegations of corruption against the ministers and others in high position. He suggested that instead of concentrating on gigantic schemes of irrigation and power, immediate results could be achieved by subsidizing small irrigation schemes undertaken with the cooperation of the farmers. If necessary, the big schemes of industrial development could be postponed in favour of investment in agriculture, he said. Towards the end of November 1959, he also wrote to the Prime Minister suggesting the appointment of a high-powered tribunal to enquire into charges against ministers and others in high positions.

Dr Rajendra Prasad retired on May 13, 1962 at the conclusion of his second term and stayed at Sadaqat Ashram in Patna. He had not been keeping well for some time. He passed away on February 28, 1963 and was cremated on the banks of Ganga in the orthodox Hindu manner.

Above all, Dr Rajendra Prasad was not only the first President of Independent India, but also the longest serving President. He was a great scholar and many universities honoured him with various doctorate degrees. He was awarded D. Litt by Patna University, LL.D by Sagar University, Mysore University and Osmania University and *Vidya Vachaspati* by the Banaras Hindu University. His most abiding qualities of character were his humility, his spirit of self-effacement and sacrifice and his total dedication to the cause of the country. Simple and unassuming in manners, he looked like a peasant. His deep penetrating eyes revealed the extraordinary sharpness of his mind. As Jawaharlal Nehru wrote; "Truth shines through those eyes". To the people, he was an ideal President, close to their own way of thinking and living. To them he was not only the Head of the State but also the fountainhead of inspiration.

6

Sarvepalli Radhakrishnan

Tenure as President
13 May 1962-13 May 1967
Votes Secured: 553,067
Nearest Rival
Ch Hari Ram
Votes Secured: 6,341

1888-1975

Dr Sarvepalli Radhakrishnan had been the second President of resurgent India. He was world's great philosopher and exponent of Hinduism with emphasis on the synthesis of Eastern and Western philosophy. He maintained that religious life does not consist in the acceptance of academic abstractions or the celebrations of ceremonies; it is spiritual certainty that provides us strength and solace in the hour of need and sorrow. His approach to philosophy is appropriately summed up in his book, *The Religion We Need*.

Born on September 5, 1888 at Tirutani, a very small temple town to the north-west of the then Madras city (now, Chennai) and the second son of a poor Brahmin couple, Sarvepalli Veeraswami and his wife, Sitamma, introspection and intellectuality could be seen from the childhood of Radhakrishnan. His father was a subordinate revenue official in the service of a local *zamindar* who found it hard to maintain his large family and send his children to school.

Radhakrishnan started his primary education from the Board High School at Tirutani at the age of four and spent about four years there, learning elementary English, Telugu, arithmetic, geography and Indian history. In 1896, he was shifted to the Mermansburg Evangelical Lutheran Mission

School at Tirupati, where he had his first lesson in the *Bible*. The study of the *Bible* came to him as a spiritual supplement to his sense of Hindu religion inculcated at home by regular practice of rituals and visits to temples. But the introduction to both the creeds was mechanical and with no noticeable impact. In school, his main activity was to play truant and walk long distances from village to village, utilizing the scholarship money he received. His parents knew no English and had no clear idea of his performance at school. But on learning of his erratic behaviour, they moved him to Vellore where his distance uncle happened to be on the teaching staff. He now drifted out of the lonely wilderness of his boyhood and his studies became more regular. After two years, he passed the matriculation examination of the University of Madras, winning scholarship. It was during the years at Vellore that he showed the first signs of enthusiasm for reading and this habit endured till the end.

While still a student at Vellore, in May 1903, at the age of 16, Radhakrishnan was married to a distant cousin, Sivakamu, aged 10. Sivakamu's father had died when Sivakamu was an infant and her mother was in no position to seek or buy for her a young man who was heir to property or of established ability.

In 1904, Radhakrishnan passed the first arts examination in the first class with distinction in mathematics, psychology and history. His choice of philosophy was later more by accident than by design. Till 1949, when public life became his primary interest, he studied philosophy with great assiduity, lectured and had written on it with breadth, fluency and vision, but it was not a study undertaken consciously. At the end of 1906, he obtained the B.A. degree with first class honours and was the best student of that year in philosophy. He thought of switching to law but this entailed financial resources which he didn't possess.

In his lectures on ethics to the M.A. classes, Hogg spoke rather disparagingly of the ascetic and other worldly tendencies of the *Bhagavad Gita*. These remarks, as well as the general atmosphere of the college, roused Radhakrishnan's interest in religious beliefs of Hindus. Impressed by the nationalist spirit which he gathered through the writings of Vivekananda he started his own search. Indian philosophy was not a part of the syllabus in Madras or indeed in any of the Indian universities, but in partial fulfillment of the requirements of the M.A. degree, he submitted his dissertation titled *The Ethics of the Vedanta and its Metaphysical Presuppositions*, which was commended for its remarkable understanding of the subject. In it he boldly and explicitly rejected the uniqueness of Christ. The life, death and resurrection of Christ were not a solitary or special portent but the supreme indication of a universal spiritual law, he maintained. Beneath the obscurantism and superstition he discerned vital sparks in the Hindu tradition—an acceptance of spiritual values and a compulsion to social service.

After obtaining M.A. degree, Radhakrishnan was appointed a Malayalam Master in the Presidency College at Madras on a salary of Rs.60. He was deputed to the Teacher's Training College at Saidapet. This was a year of real hardship for him, as Radhakrishnan's household, on one occasion, was unable to afford even the banana leaves on which food is served in South India. He auctioned his university medals and borrowed money. Later, when he was unable to clear his debts in 1913 he was dragged to court in a civil suit. He started doing private tuitions, checked answer papers for the university and wrote a textbook, *Essentials of Psychology*, printed by Clarendon Press in Oxford. He sold all the rights to the publisher for Rs.500.

Later, Radhakrishnan worked in Presidency College first as additional professor and then as assistant professor of philosophy. His reputation for clarity and comprehensiveness was so widespread that students of other colleges also attended his classes. Apart from the study of philosophy, teaching and an active social life, Radhakrishnan took interest in English literature. His favourite authors were: Plato, Aristotle, Augustine, Kant, Locke, Mill, Chaucer, Blake, Longfellow, Plutarch, Carlyle and Darwin. As a result, what attracted the lay readers to Radhakrishnan's learned works was not only the smooth handling of the English language and the vigour and clarity of the style but also the literary allusions and the striking quotations from creative writers. During the years at the Presidency College he learnt Sanskrit with the help of *pandits* and then studied the classics, the Upanishads and the *Bhagavad Gita* as well as the commentaries on them. He also read in English the Buddhist texts as well as those of Jainism.

In 1915, Radhakrishnan studied Rabindranath Tagore. He felt irritated by the claims made in the West that Tagore's outlook was deeply influenced by Christianity. He spelt out Tagore's outlook that in essence he was a Hindu Vedantist in line with the thinkers of the Vedas and the Upanishads. To Radhakrishnan, Tagore's work was the outcome and expression of the Indian ideals of philosophy, religion and art. In 1920, his book, *The Reign of Religion in Contemporary Philosophy*, was well acclaimed and prescribed in a number of British and American universities for providing a clear and able exposition and discussion of the fundamentals of contemporary philosophy. He planned a series of novels depicting the changing India.

In 1923, George Allen & Unwin brought out his massive work, *Indian Philosophy*, in two volumes. His endeavour was to expound Indian thought in terms which related it to the Western tradition. He felt that ignorance in other countries of the philosophy of India was mainly due to the unattractive clothing in which it was put. He tried to avoid jargon to explain the special terms used in Indian texts which were not easily rendered into English. He said that the thinkers of ancient India had grappled with the basic problems of life and formulated theories which had not lost their value. He, therefore, discussed these theories in terms of modern thought and related them to the living issues of philosophy and religion without substitution of current arguments for ancient lines of thought.

When Radhakrishnan joined Calcutta (now, Kolkatta) in March 1921, the students were on strike at the call of Mahatma Gandhi. Radhakrishnan's sympathy was against the authorities. In an article on "Gandhi and Tagore", written under a pseudonym, because he was still a government servant, he accepted that Gandhi was the great living person because of his spiritual ideals but was unenthusiastic about a political campaign that assumed all its followers to be heroes, an economic programme that required the burning and boycott of foreign cloth, and, above all, an educational policy that called on students to leave schools and colleges. But when Mahatma Gandhi called off the campaign of civil disobedience because of the burning of a few policemen by a riotous mob, Radhakrishnan was convinced that Gandhi's movement was deeply spiritual and that non-cooperation was a war of principle waged with the strength of the spirit, and that to cooperate with the British Government was to submit to sin and to take up the sword to stab the soul. Gandhi, according to Radhakrishnan, applied religion to politics and sought to convert the world of nations to the higher law of love.

Radhakrishnan suggested that Christianity, if properly understood, had much in common with the fundamentals of Hindu thought. He said that Christianity should help Hinduism to enrich its spirit not by giving of itself but by helping Hinduism to discover what lay in it undelivered. He felt, what humanity needed was not conversion to a single faith or a pale syncretism but an intelligent understanding of the deeper unity of principle among all religions, as the misunderstanding of almost all the religions is due to a false sense of a monopoly of truth.

In 1926, Radhakrishnan was invited to deliver Upton Lectures at the Congress of Universities in England. It provided him an opportunity to present to a non-Hindu audience the fundamentals of the Hindu religion. These lectures were later published under the title *Hindu View of Life*.

From 1931 to 1939, Radhakrishnan was Vice-Chancellor of Andhra University. His reputation as scholar and speaker led to requests from various universities for the delivery of convocation addresses. At these addresses, he reminded the audience that freedom was won from within and not given from without. The students should not renounce the Indian tradition but adapt it to modern needs. Association between India and Britain, ne said, could become an expression of the ultimate synthesis between the East and the West if both sides acted upon their responsibilities. At Lahore, he stressed that universities should train the young for leadership. In June 1931, he was honoured with knighthood by the British Government for his recognition as a philosopher. But when Mahatma Gandhi, at the conclusion of Second Round Table Conference, returned disappointed, Radhakrishnan paid his 'homage of love' to Gandhi for his example of self-respect and moral courage. He defined the duty of universities to be the handling of the lighted torch of culture, which stirs upheavals and starts conflagrations.

In the summer of 1936, Radhakrishnan was in Britain till the outbreak of war in September 1939. There he spoke with authority on India's culture and her problems. On political issues, he continued to support the leadership of Mahatma Gandhi. His lectures at Oxford were devoted to comparative religion and influence, in the past, of Indian thought on Greece, Rome and Palestine. Being a good lecturer and imbued with a striking personality, he drew students from various disciplines even though the subject had little to do with examination syllabi, and his audiences were of a respectable size. To many senior members of the university too the very presence of Radhakrishnan offered the prospect of new approaches to traditional subjects and unexpected insights in well-traversed fields of study.

Dr Radhakrishnan accepted the responsibility of Banaras Hindu University as its Vice Chancellor at a time when it was in a critical financial situation. With his flair for a quick seizure of any issue and for rapid decision and ability to delegate authority to the right persons, he toned up the administration. He himself undertook extensive tours of the country to collect funds. As a result, within two years of his taking up the vice chancellorship a quarter of the debt was wiped off and donations were procured for specific purposes, e.g. buildings and fellowship.

In May 1944, Radhakrishnan had been to China for two weeks to deliver lectures on Buddhism and Religion. When Constituent Assembly came into existence, the senior leaders of the Congress unhesitatingly invited Radhakrishnan to be one of the non-Congressmen who would be put up by the

Party for election to the Assembly. On attaining Independence, in his midnight speech on the night of August 14, 1947 he counseled his countrymen to develop the tolerant attitude and see in fellow beings the face Divine.

Radhakrishnan's edition of the *Bhagavad Gita* was published in the spring of 1948. In his Introduction and notes he emphasized that the *Gita* contained the natural elements of true religion. The *Gita*, as he interpreted, emphasized both the personal and the social sides of spiritual religion. The highest perfection, he said, is a combination of knowledge, devotion and work, not renunciation of action but action with renunciation of desire. The aim of religion, he emphasized, is not just individual salvation but the establishment of a brotherhood upon earth.

After Independence, Prime Minister Jawaharlal Nehru looked upon Radhakrishnan as the most clear-headed authority on education in India. He was asked to head a Commission to study the working of universities in India in all its aspects with a view to recommend measures for their improvement. The Commission regarded as its chief task the elucidation of the principles on which highest education should be recast to meet the changing needs and conditions of a free country. The Commission visited all the universities, met in Shimla and produced a long and comprehensive report. The Commission recommended that the Constitution list the university education as a concurrent subject so that the Central Government could intervene to ensure national standards whenever the necessity arose. It proposed the establishment of University Grants Commission. It urged an enhancement of the salaries of teachers both to raise their social status and to improve their quality.

In April 1949, Dr Radhakrishnan was appointed India's Ambassador in Moscow, where he saw himself as not just the Ambassador of India concerned with bilateral relations but as the spokesman of humanity at large. There his task was one of reconciliation and understanding, understand the Soviet policies and interpret and make the Soviet authorities understand India's policies.

In 1952, Dr Radhakrishnan was appointed Vice President of India. He was elected President in May 1962, as the official candidate of the Congress. During his tenure as President, the erstwhile Viceroy's residence in Shimla, which had hardly been used after Mountbatten's departure, was transferred to the Ministry of Education to house an Institute of Advanced Study which Dr Radhakrishnan wanted to develop on the lines of Princeton or All Souls. He also initiated the process of throwing open the gates of the President's palace in Delhi twice a week to whosoever might wish to present petitions and voice grievances.

In October 1962, during China's aggression, Dr Radhakrishnan's rapidly moving mind proved to be an asset. He directed the then Defence Minister, Krishna Menon, to bring the three Chiefs of Staff with him to explain the situation to the conference of governors then meeting in New Delhi. He suggested to Jawaharlal Nehru that Menon be moved from the Defence Ministry. He met the generals in command, went to the forward areas, and talked to the troops in retreat after the first round of Chinese attacks. As President, he regarded himself as above government and party and the spokesman of public feelings. He even publicly acknowledged the 'credulity and negligence' of government which had brought matters to this stage. Such outspokenness by the Head of State in India was unprecedented—a philosopher with a moral authority.

On Nehru's death on May 27, 1964, everyone turned to the President for guidance and decision. He became a much loved elder uncle who understood everybody's problems. He helped to hold the people together, supported the Government's policies, assisted in their proper implementation and did not allow the larger vision to be forgotten. In view of some developments, including the annoyance caused to the Prime Minister by his outspokenness he resolved to retire and did not allow his name to be considered for extension. After retirement in May 1967 he returned to Madras.

In Madras, though surrounded by the affection of his family, life appeared to him joyless. He was lonely in mind and spirit. His vitality ran low. A succession of minor strokes followed. In September 1973, he slipped and broke his hip. Thereafter, he was bed-ridden with neither the will to live nor the ability to die. It lingered on, slowly losing his mental faculties and moving in and out of a nursing home with a succession of complaints. Just then a Templeton Prize for Progress was announced for him. He transferred the prize money to Oxford University. Finally, on April 17, 1975, Radhakrishnan's curtain of life was drawn.

Finally, with his belief in God, Radhakrishnan was confident from his earliest years that he was singled out for great achievement. To him, as to Bertrand Russell, philosophy was an effort to find the meaning of life, and like Russell he had an analytical skill. He developed the discipline of comparative religion with a view to bringing to the forefront the moral values and spiritual insight common to all organized religions. To Western readers, he interpreted the philosophy of India in a language intelligible to them. The commitment to society, the crusading, urgent tone in his scholarly writings, the modern note in his interpretation of even classical texts, and his intellectual resistance to the deforming pressures of colonialism gave him even in the late twenties a distinct public image. His political awareness awakened him to social injustice. Above all, Dr Radhakrishnan emerged clearly as one of the great transformative personalities of our age.

7

Zakir Husain

Tenure as President
13 May 1967-3 May 1969
Votes Secured: 471,244
Nearest Rival
K. Subba Rao
Votes Secured: 363,971

1897-1969

Dr Zakir Husain, the third President of India, was a born educationist, though an economist by training. He took Mahatma Gandhi's ideas and gave them an educational thrust through appropriate techniques. He said, "Gandhiji with the intuitive grasp of reality, characteristic of genius, made handiwork an integral part of our education as the medium of instruction for boys and girls up to the age of 14. I wonder if he realized that by doing so he made Indian education conscious of a fundamental truth which it would ignore only at its own peril. He did not work out his ideas theoretically." Like Rousseau, Comenius, Pestalozzi, Kerschensteiner and Dewey, he realized the educational potentialities of work. Following Kerschensteiner, Dr Zakir Husain was fully convinced that education can be imparted only through 'doing'. He emphasized that learning by doing is more effective and permanent. A keen observer of child behaviour, a voracious reader, a gifted speaker, one of the most creative thinkers of education of contemporary India, Dr Zakir Husain evolved the best of his energies to the problems of proper and adequate education.

Born on February 8, 1897, Zakir Husain was the third son of Fida Husain Khan and Nazreen. His father studied law and practiced it. His mother was quite a courageous lady. The boy was brought up in an upper class Muslim atmosphere with all its inherent customs and traditions. During his childhood, it was considered to be against the dignity of the family to allow him to cross the street in front of his house on foot or to come out of the house without being properly dressed. In his speech, manners and even in his sartorial choice, therefore, he exhibited a rare and refined taste.

In 1905, when Zakir Husain was barely nine-years old and was studying in Sultan Bazar Government High School in Hyderabad, his father died of tuberculosis at the young age of 39. In 1908, he was sent to a residential school in Etawah called the Islamia High School. Here he learnt the imperative need to sacrifice physical pleasures for the higher values of life. Syed Altar Husain, who was headmaster of the school, advised him to remember "that one could not enjoy life and still excel in the performance of duty". The boy remembered this throughout his life. He showed a great interest in current affairs. Everyday, he would walk all the way to Etawah railway station to get the first available copy of *The Pioneer* and then run back to his friends waiting at the boarding house to read aloud to them the important news of the day interspersed with his own comments. While in school, he came in close contact with several nationalist leaders who awakened in him a sense of social awareness and created in him a lasting interest in national and international affairs which helped in moulding the future course of his life.

The impact of his mother's influence on Zakir Husain was profound. It is said that temperamentally the son had taken after the mother. He even observed before his own children that it was due to the deep influence of his mother that he became conscious of his duties towards his fellow countrymen, irrespective of any consideration of caste, creed or religion. After his mother's death, Zakir Husain came under the influence of a Sufi saint, Hasan Shah. He would copy out whole books for him as Hasan Shah could not afford to buy the books, and thereby, he not only developed a good handwriting but also a sound knowledge of Persian, and widened the horizons of his knowledge and interests. The humanistic principles of communal harmony and universal brotherhood, his generosity and open-mindedness, his characteristic modesty, his qualities of head and heart, and even his fondness for calligraphy and interest in Persian manuscripts, all have their roots in the benevolent influence of his broad-minded and noble mother. The spiritual guidance of Hasan Shah, reinforced by the healthy influence of Syed Altaf Husain, and the family atmosphere inherited from his grandfather, Ghulam Husain Khan guided his future life and actions.

After passing the matriculation examination in 1913 with distinction, Zakir Husain joined the Mohammedian Anglo-Oriental College at Aligarh from where he passed the intermediate examination in Science with Biology. While still an undergraduate student, he was married to Shahjahan Begum. He passed the B.A. examination in 1918 with first division, securing a position among the first four and winning the coveted Iqbal Medal. As a postgraduate student, he took up economics and law and was appointed a junior lecturer. He was also elected the Vice President of the students union and was a formidable debater, winning many prizes. He regularly contributed to the college magazine under the pen-name of 'Rip'.

In October 1920, Mahatma Gandhi asked the students and teachers to boycott Government and Government-aided institutions. At the same time, at Aligarh, an enthusiastic group was anxious to see that the MAO College did not become a British Government University. Sensing the demand of a number of people for a national institution, Jamia Milia institution was established on October 29, 1920 in the college mosque. Zakir Husain joined it as a lecturer in Economics. On November 22, 1920, the Jamia Milia Islamia was given proper form with a Board of Trustees, an Executive Committee, an Academic Council, a Chancellor, Vice-Chancellor, pro-Vice Chancellor, and Principal of the College, Secretary and Registrar. Soon, it developed into an educational complex with a primary school, secondary school, adult education centre, training college, Art College, library and publication department, etc.

While in Jamia Milia Islamia, Zakir Husain gained the maximum practical experience as a practicing educationist. It was here that he tried to build a healthy synthesis between religious aims and national aims of education. His experiences at the Jamia taught him that if Muslims were not given the right to make their culture the basis of their education, it would be a source of weakness and prove to be an obstacle in the path of progress. He approached the Muslim masses through adult education programmes of the Jamia Milia, breaking through the social cordon of class. To practice social equality, National Week (April 7 to 13) was celebrated in Jamia Milia every year, and on the last day all the work usually done by hostel servants, peons, cooks, sweepers, was taken over by the staff and students to inculcate in them the feeling of respect for duty in the former and the sense of dignity of labour in the latter. The week concluded with a community dinner in which all high and low sat and ate together. Night schools were started for the illiterate people. Project Method laws were initiated at the lower level and the Activity Method at the secondary level. A number of ideas about education were discussed in all their aspects to keep the institution free from the domination of any political part. In this way, Jamia Milia became an embodiment of Dr Zakir Husain's educational ideas.

In 1922, Zakir Husain left for Germany to join the University of Berlin to do his Ph.D. In Germany, he met Mohammed Mujeeb and Abid Husain who were so impressed with him and his devotion to the Jamia Milia that they promised life long service to the institution. The welfare of the Jamia Milia was his prime concern even in Germany. When he was informed that due to financial crisis Jamia was on the brink of closure, he sent a telegram to its organizers asking them to keep it going somehow till his return. In 1926, he submitted his thesis on *The Agricultural Economy of India* under Prof. Werner Sombart. His stay in Germany gave him a broader outlook of human affairs and he imbibed the efficiency and thoroughness of approach of the Germans. He also acquired an interest in and developed an appreciation of Western classical music and modern art. There he also arranged the publication of the *Diwan-e-Ghalib* at the Kaviani Press, Berlin, which he himself partly composed for the Maktaba Jamia. He also toured the Scandinavian countries to further enrich his experiences.

On his return to India, Dr Zakir Husain found the Jamia Milia Islamia in bad shape. He, therefore, assumed the duties of the Shaik-ul-Jamia and with his courage, foresight, dedication and qualities of leadership, he overcame the obstacles and the Jamia blossomed with the blessings of Mahatma Gandhi. In the autumn of 1937, Dr Zakir Husain attended the National Educational Conference held at Wardha. Mahatma Gandhi was so impressed with Dr Zakir Husain's reaction to his own proposed scheme, which was backed by his experience in the field of national education, that he nominated him as the President of the Committee formed to draft the resolutions. After the Conference was over, a Committee was also constituted by Mahatma Gandhi with Dr Zakir Husain as its Chairman, to prepare a syllabus of the scheme of Basic Education. After that Dr Zakir Husain was closely associated with *Nai Talim*.

According to Dr Zakir Husain, 'work' is that activity of man which has a definite objective. It aims at concrete objective realization of some ideas and is of great educative value. But all work is not educative. In India, a majority of our people do hard work, strenuous physical work, but all are not educated. Only educative work, he felt, constitutes the real source of true education. In his view, educative work is that which helps in the cultivation of the mind and in the shaping of character and personality. He said that educative work must issue forth from some mental activity. An activity can be called educative only if it is preceded by some mental comprehension or understanding of what has to be imitated, attained or achieved. He said that educative work does not become educative by itself unless the student earnestly aims it as perfect an attainment as possible from the point of view of its result. "Unfinished, careless, slipshod work, whatsoever else it might be, is surely not educative", he said.

Dr Zakir Husain put forth four characteristic stages of educative work. First, the learner must gain clear consciousness of the work-activity to be pursued, and he should be made fully aware of what exactly is to be done. Secondly, he should be involved in the development of the plan of work, which includes the choice of appropriate means, breaking up the educative work into various steps by which it can be accomplished. In the third stage, the work is actually executed and in the fourth, the result of the work is thoroughly assessed. It involves self-criticism and self-appraisal which are necessary for further improvement. Dr Zakir Husain's concept of educational work, mental and intellectual activities is an integral part of work at all its stages. Therefore, he emphasized that learning by doing is more effective and permanent.

He emphasized that the learner has to be given the skill of careful, self-critical and methodical process of thinking. If the learner is not given enough opportunities to practice logical thinking, he tends to develop the habits of gullible credibility of suspicious incredulousness. The opportunity to practice logical thinking, he said, is provided by the essential mental constituent of educative work. Skill, he said, is of two types: mechanical skill, attained by imitative diligence, capable of regarding existing values, or non-mechanical skill based on natural disposition, creating new values. The first kind of skill is an exterior addition and, the second kind is an enrichment and transformation within. It is the second type of mental skill which has to be constantly reinforced by traditional knowledge and mechanical skill.

Dr Zakir Husain was greatly influenced by Hegel. Hegelism was reigning supreme in Germany in the days when Dr Zakir Husain was studying in Berlin University. He was convinced that the society or the State assumes a kind of parental status for man's spiritual being and for making him integrally self-conscious. He believed that human being cannot exist in a vacuum and depends for his existence on society and his individual mind is rooted in the social mind. Keeping the deep-seated individual-society relationship in view, Dr Zakir Husain believed that education must provide for free and full development of individual and social excellence of every educated man to make an excellent human society. The aim of education, therefore, must be to secure for every person such conditions which are conducive to his total individual development. But he said that too much importance to the individual might endanger the cohesion of the society as it will make the individual a selfish member of society. Similarly, too much emphasis on society will strengthen the totalitarian nature of the society. Nevertheless, he wanted education to develop in every individual his sense of discrimination between good and bad ideas of individual life. Therefore, he wanted education to develop human faculties in order to enable an individual to discharge his duties towards the society successfully and faithfully, treating education as the most powerful instrument of social change.

Dr Zakir Husain was a deeply religious man. He highlighted the significance of service of man, regardless of distinction of caste and creed, communal harmony, sectional selflessness, love for humanity, eradication of every type of slavery, etc. He wanted the Islamic schools to be conducted on principles and Muslims to be men of character coupled with scientific attitude towards life as well as firm religious faith and conviction in the spiritual dimension of human life. He treated religious values in the broader perspective of humanity and total human upliftment. He gave great importance to generosity, benevolence and hospitality and treated them in truly religious values. This follows that Dr Zakir Husain made national service, moral values and even physical and material values integral to religious values and ideals for a truly cultured man. Through education he wanted to prepare men of character, to help them develop free, moral personalities. He said that "from individuality through character to personality is the destiny of worthy human life".

After Independence, Dr Zakir Husain was appointed Vice Chancellor of Aligarh Muslim University. Under his leadership, the University earned an enviable reputation for itself in all walks of academic and extra-curricular activities. In 1957, he was offered the governorship of Bihar. He remained Governor till 1962. In 1962, he was elected Vice-President of India. As an ex-officio Chairman of the Rajya Sabha he guided the deliberations of the august House for five years with great dignity, tact, impartiality, patience and understanding. Even during the turbulent Question Hour in Rajya Sabha, he seldom raised his voice and yet managed to maintain dignity and decorum in the House. As a statesman he commanded great respect, both at home and abroad. His interest in flowers, plants, trees, fossils, rocks, painting, calligraphy, literature, science, technology, and education helped him to interact with people all over the world.

He was selected President of India in 1967. As President, on the occasion of the International Inter-Religious Symposium on Peace, held in New Delhi in January 1968, he said: "We want peace between individuals and groups within nations and peace among the nations. These are all vitally interdependent. If Buddha's philosophy of compassion, the Hindu concept of *Ahimsa* and the passion of Islam for obedience to the will of God can combine, then we shall see generated the most potent influence for world peace.". Diplomats and statesmen from far and near, during their meeting with him, felt the nobility of his presence and his ideas.

While in the Rashtrapati Bhavan he breathed his last on May 3, 1969. He was buried in the Jamia Milia where he became 'one with the soil, flowers and the plants of the land' he had nourished. Both as Vice-President and President of India, Dr Zakir Husain brought great erudition, elegance and eminence to the high office. Members of Parliament, Ministers and official all uniformly respected him for his catholicity of his outlook.

Dr Zakir Husain had been a keen observer of child behaviour and was fully conversant with the various genres employed in the history of story-telling for children. He believed that children's stories constitute a permanent form of literature and one can, indeed, say quite a lot through them. The themes of his stories for children were relevant to the socio-political conditions of those times. He tried to teach the simple values of freedom, courage, honesty, mother's selfless love, kindness to animals, charity, love, and faith in God. His stories have also elements of nationalism, like the boycott of foreign goods, evil of foreign rule, shortcomings of dominion status, etc., which he used in building up the plots of these stories.

Above all, Dr Zakir Husain was a creative educationist. He presented a plan of education that could save our children from rickety theoretical education imposed on us by the colonial rule. He was a man of deep culture, scholarship and a symbol of India's heritage and wisdom. We need to imbibe his qualities.

8

Justice Mohammed Hidayatullah

Tenure as Acting President
20 July 1969-24 August 1969

1905-1992

Justice Mohammed Hidayatullah held distinguished offices in India. He had been a Senior Government Pleader, Advocate General, Chief Justice of High Court, Chief Justice of Supreme Court, Vice President of India, and Acting President of India. He was a highly disciplined person and had a resilient mind passionately devoted to the Rule of Law and refinement of the human mind. His life brings to focus the history of thought, particularly sociological thought. It is the history of continuous displacement of erroneous dogma.

Justice Hidayatullah belonged to a middle class literary Muslim family. It hailed from Benaras. His grandfather was from *Chishti* descent. Beef was a taboo as the pork was. He was the son of Khan Bahadur Hafiz Mohammad Wilayatullah, I.S.W, *Kaiser-I-Hind*. His father, who was a magistrate, had become a *Hafiz* (one who knows the *Quran* by heart) at the age of nine and was a recipient of many medals. The Government recognized his services and he received the title of *Khan Bahadur*, the *Kaiser-I-Hind*, the Indian Service Order and the Badge of St. John's Ambulance. His mother, Mohammadi Begum, was barely literate. As she belonged to a religious family she was in strict *purdah* (veil).

Mohammed Hidayatullah was born on December 17, 1905 in Nagpur. At the age of five he was enrolled in the Anjuman High School. He found the life in school colourless. There was no provision for extracurricular activities in this school. When his father was shifted to other places, the boy had to change his schools. In this way, he changed eight schools within a span of twelve years. He studied in Morris College in Nagpur from 1922 to 1926, where he pursued English Literature, English History, European History, Logic and Persian. After doing graduation, he went to London where he was admitted in Trinity College in 1927. While in London, he became interested in speaking in public. He delivered a lecture at Hyde Park Corner when the Simon Commission was being boycotted in India. He participated in debates. He also began free-lance journalism and short-story writing. He joined Law Tripos. In 1929, he passed the Bar Final examination and was called to the Bar from Lincoln's Inn on January 13, 1930. Earlier, while pursuing for the English Tripos he felt interested in drama. The first play he saw was Agatha Christie's *Murder of Sir Roger Ackroyd*. Many others followed it.

The legal profession was not his first choice. His major interest was in literature. However, he took the bar examination as a *tour de force* to keep himself busy in London. However, on return to India he enrolled himself as an Advocate in the Judicial Commissioner's Court at Nagpur. In the beginning, as it was the practice during those days, he had the support of seniors. His first paid brief was a case under section 145 of the Code of Criminal Procedure under which a criminal case is started by the police or private party to get back possession of immovable property. The witnesses appeared but he was handicapped, as he did not know Marathi. He asked his colleague to help him who was unprepared and the cross-examination was ineffective. He lost the case. Later, he filed a civil suit and got the order set aside. He studied criminal law thoroughly. He read the leading statutes on the subject. He also thoroughly went through cases of Privy Council and summarized them. He read every Full Bench case of the Judicial Commissioner's Court. Gradually, his reputation was established. He got the first break in a sensational case called *The Dhantoli Abduction* case and thereafter had many more briefs.

After four years at the Bar, Hidayatullah also worked as a part-time lecturer in the Nagpur University. He taught jurisprudence and Mahomedian Law. He also taught Constitutional Law, Torts, Contract and Succession Act till he became a Government Pleader. Though he was at the forefront in Criminal Law, he found that Civil Law had more scope for developing legal acumen. A number of criminal cases established his reputation and he had to work hard to prepare the cases. He had an opportunity to work with leading legal luminaries like Sir Tej Bahadur Sapru and Sir C.P. Ramaswamy.

He was a Government Pleader in 1942 for nine months before becoming the Advocate General for the Central Provinces and the Berar Government. The Government Pleaders were required to look after the cases in courts dividing the work among them. The Advocate General gave opinions to Government and conducted some important cases. He was the Senior Government Pleader. He was Advocate General from 1943 to 1956.

On June 13, 1946, he was granted the dignity of an Additional Officer of the Civil Division of the Order of British Empire. It was given to him because of his exceptional services as Advocate General. He was appointed High Court Judge in 1946 and remained there till 1954. He was sworn in as acting Judge of Nagpur High Court on June 24, 1946 and again on August 13, 1946 as permanent judge. In 1954, he was sworn in as Chief Justice of the Nagpur High Court.

On May 5, 1948, Justice Hidayatullah married Pushpa, the eldest daughter of A.N. Shah, ICS, Chairman of All-India Income Tax Appellate Tribunal. This was an inter-religious marriage but the affection the couple received belied their fears of ostracism. Their son, Arshad, was born after a year and in 1952, Pushpa gave birth to a girl child, Avni. Arshad became an advocate. In 1954, Justice Hidayatullah took his family to Europe. In Paris, he witnessed the 400th anniversary of Versailles. The couple had a red carpet treatment.

Soon after his return, Justice Hidayatullah officiated for a fortnight as acting Chief Justice and shortly afterwards was appointed permanent Chief Justice. During his tenure as Chief Justice, he had been to some of the Districts under the High Court. As Chief Justice he received the unstinted cooperation of all his colleagues. He handled a sensational case with Justice Kotval. The Government of Madhya Pradesh had appointed a Committee of Enquiry with Sir Bhawani Shankar Niyogi as chairman to report on the activities of Christian Missions. One Francis challenged this as opposed to the guarantees of religious freedom in the Constitution. The Christians of India were much agitated. The decision of this case put a great strain on Justice Hidayatullah. He worked hard to produce a written judgment, which dealt with Public Inquiries the world over and the views taken about them by courts, lawyers and writers. It was appealed against but the Supreme Court declined to interfere. Christian bulletins and books all over the world quoted extracts from his judgment.

Because of reorganization of the States in 1956, Justice Hidayatullah had now the responsibility of dividing the judicial services. The High Court was shifted to Jabalpur and its shifting posed many problems. They included the division of cases according to the original place of jurisdiction, the personnel and the division of property. If a case had begun at a place within the future jurisdiction of the Jabalpur High Court it was to be retained on file there otherwise it had to be transferred to the Bombay High Court. The Hindi-speaking personnel were engaged in Jabalpur High Court while those speaking Marathi were shifted to Bombay. Allotment of an existing building, its renovation to suit the work of the High Court and its furnishing was itself a stupendous task, involving the personal attention of Justice Hidayatullah.

Justice Hidayatullah left for Bhopal on October 30, 1956 to administer the oath of office to the Governor of Madhya Pradesh. When elections took place, he came across a spate of election appeals. Each case required good deal of scrutiny and over this he did not have the full sanctioned strength. He carried on with the full cooperation of his colleagues and the Bar, and managed not only to keep abreast of the fresh institutions but also made a big dent in the number of the pending cases with special reference to the old cases. He requested the Bar that there should be no request to adjourn an old case. All old cases were shown at the top of the court's daily docket. If they were adjourned they appeared at the head of the list in the next week. In this way, he was able to weed out the old cases. Another method that he devised was to get compiled a list for disposal of cases each week separately for each judge and also the number of cases he heard at the admission stage, the number admitted to hearing, the number dismissed *in limine* and the number adjourned. With this list went a list of cases heard by any judge and pending for judgment with the date on which he reserved judgment. A Special Officer sent these in a sealed cover, with copies of figures of each court. There was a remarkable increase in disposals. This, he felt, was the ideal *modus* for speeding up cases. A Special Officer was asked to group cases according to the subject matter. This saved time of the judges who had not to switch their minds from one law to another. The cases filed bore the number of the case and the subject in brackets. Another device to save time was in relation to Letters Patent Appeals. The judge granting leave would himself fix a date before the Chief Justice who would give a date for hearing before a Division Bench. In the meantime, parties exchanged the memorandum of appeal or cross-objection, as the case may be. This avoided much delay. All these efforts bore fruit and the figures compiled for his court, class-wise, subject-wise and age-wise by the Special Officer every month bore all this.

During his term of two years as Chief Justice of the composite Madhya Pradesh he recommended many judges for appointment. He discouraged all attempts to regard judges from Part B and C States as in any way inferior to judges from Part A State. As a result of the existing prejudice, most of the brightest judges in the past had never reached the High

Court Bench. In his State, he assured fair play to all. He asked each judge to choose three of the cases decided by him, which he considered his best performances. The Registrar chose three others. These were placed before him for his inspection. The Chief Justice himself scrutinized them carefully, called some for interview and graded them through his confidential reports. They kept their places in the combined seniority list but their future increments, promotions, postings, etc. depended on his confidential reports. Some were warned and some were told that they were being watched for promotion either to the High Court or as District Judges. No *ad hoc* advantage was given or preference shown to the judges. When the lower Bench knew this they appreciated this fair play. With the help of his Registrar Justice Hidayatullah spent his whole vacation at Indore, reading the enormous material to grade the judges. Two of his senior-most colleagues were always at hand to see the best, the worst and doubtful cases so that he himself had not only his judgment but also of theirs.

When Justice S.R. Das was the Chief Justice of India in 1957, Justice Hidayatullah was elevated as Judge of the Supreme Court. The hearing of cases in the highest court was altogether a different experience to him. Here he found the environment much different. In Supreme Court, he became a member of the Constitution Bench, but he did most of the tax or criminal cases. He was a puisne judge in the Supreme Court for just over nine years before he became Chief Justice on February 25, 1968. The very first case he heard was *State of Rajasthan v Chawla*, A.I.R, 1959 S.C, 544, and it was decided whether the power to regulate the use of loud amplifiers in public places flowed from List II entry No.1 (Public Order) and/or entry No.6 (Public Health). He thought that 'Health' was not as appropriate as Public Order in the larger sense, having regard to the problem of music before mosques, but one of his colleagues did not agree. He realized then that it would not be easy to get over the opposition. In *Mahadeo v. Bombay* (A.I.R. 1959 S.C. 735), where he wished to overrule *Chhotabhai*'s case (A.I.R.1953, S.C.108) and gave full reasons, the Chief Justice asked him to leave them out. In *Lord Krishna Sugar Mills* case (A.I..R,1959, S.C.1124) he gave his dissent. He heard the *Berubari* case (A.I.R.1960 S.C.845), which was a President Reference. He gave a separate opinion. Similarly, in many other cases, he was content to give his own opinion and leave others free to accept his point of view or not. The most important of these was the famous case, *Golaknath v. State of Punjab* A.I.R, 1967 S.C.1943.

In 1965, Justice Hidayatullah attended the Conference of the International Commission of Jurists and in 1967 he attended the General Assembly of the International Fellowship of Former Scouts and Guides at Durham as the Guest of Honour. In 1965, he delivered the Lajpat Rai Memorial Lectures. His lectures were published in a book entitled *Democracy in India and the Judicial Process*. On April 27, 1964, he was invited to speak at the Fourth Birth Centenary of Shakespeare and he chose *Shakespeare, the Man and the Legend* as the subject. On July 1, 1967, the Institute of Constitutional and Parliamentary Studies invited him to speak on *Parliamentary Privileges: The Press and the Judiciary*.

Justice Hidayatullah was sworn in as Chief Justice of India on February 25, 1968. The first sad incident was an attack on his life as well as of his colleagues, Justice Grover and Justice Vaidyalingam by Man Mohan Das, an ex-sailor from the Merchant Navy, while Justice Hidayatullah was presiding over a bench. Justice Hidayatullah showed an exemplary presence of mind and courage when he grabbed the assailant. Justice Grover was wounded. He received the highest award for gallantry (the Bronze Medal) from the Boy Scouts Association, which President Zakir Husain presented to him at a colourful ceremony. Before this, on November 19, 1948, he had already received the highest award, the Silver Elephant, and in 1946, the War Service Badge from the Association.

When President Dr Zakir Husain suddenly expired, V.V. Giri was sworn in as the Acting President. For the post of President, the Congress Party nominated Sanjiva Reddy. Giri, the Acting President, was not chosen although two Vice-Presidents had been chosen earlier. Giri resigned as Acting President to contest for the seat of President of India and Justice Hidayatullah was sworn in as Acting President of India on July 20, 1969. During his tenure as Acting President of India, the Ambassador-designate to Sudan and Mrs Dalal met him. Kenneth Keating, Ambassador for the United States visited him. A Money Bill, about to be introduced in the Lok Sabha, was brought before him. Under Article 117 of the Constitution, such a Bill cannot be introduced or moved unless the President recommends it. This is a mere formality. He summoned Dr Nagendra Singh and questioned him. He was shocked to find that while both the Houses of Parliament were expected to pass the Bill before sending it to the President, it had not yet been moved even. Justice Hidayatullah, however, corrected it and signed a recommendation. There was a debate in the Rajya Sabha initiated by Raj Narain that as the letter of resignation was sent by V.V. Giri to the Prime Minister, it had no validity and therefore there was no vacancy, which Justice Hidayatullah could fill. The Vice-Chairman, M.P. Bhargava, ruled that Justice Hidayatullah was functioning constitutionally. A representation was made to him that the election of the Speaker of the Lok Sabha was being 'needlessly delayed.' He directed that the election be held without delay.

The schism in the Ruling Party (Congress) and the resignation of Morarji Desai as the Deputy Prime Minister raised some rumours that Prime Minister Indira Gandhi had lost her majority in the Lok Sabha and that she would advice the President to dissolve the Lok Sabha. Justice Hidayatullah, who was now the President of India, began looking up precedents, both of English and India. But the occasion to exercise this power did not arise at all and he had no occasion to use his judgment. He promulgated the laws applicable to Laccadive and the other Islands. He also greeted and congratulated the three astronauts who had successfully conducted a voyage to the moon and back. He accepted the appeal of the Deans of Benares Hindu University in his capacity as Visitor of the University, and allowed them to express freely their views on the Gajendragadkar Committee's report on the University. When the Bank Nationalization Bill was passed he had a deputation of Members of Parliament who opposed it. He told them plainly that a Bill passed *nem con* in the two Houses could not be stopped unless there was a good reason. He promised to look into the provisions carefully before giving his assent. He studied Giri's Ordinance and compared the Bill with the Ordinance to see if any changes had been made. Then he examined the provisions to see if there were provisions for compensation, proper take over and vesting of assets and particularly if there were proper safeguards for the depositors, creditors and debtors, etc. After satisfying himself that there was no reason for returning the Bill, he assented to it. He knew that the peoples' representatives had passed the Bill without a single dissenting vote. Unless it was wrong intrinsically or offended the Constitution or procedural rules, the President was bound to assent to it. That is how he decided this issue.

On August 1, 1969, he received and welcomed President Nixon. When President Nixon asked him what help India expected to control its population President Hidayatullah told the visiting President that India needed a great number of mobile vans equipped with mass-media communication systems and clinical facilities so that work of family planning in villages could be undertaken. Both the Presidents also discussed the problem of population growth in detail. They also discussed about the judicial systems of the two countries. He addressed the nation on Independence Day. When V.V. Giri was elected President of India, he exchanged places and resumed his normal routine as Chief Justice of India, thereby showing that he had only been the President *pro-tempore*.

After resuming office of the Chief Justice of India, he had before him a decision of the Punjab High Court in appeal. Justice Hidayatullah departed from the convention. He requested the judges to return during the summer vacation to convene a Bench of five judges to hear the case. The urgency arose because the whole democratic process had come to a halt by the action of the Speaker in adjourning the Legislative Assembly on the eve of the budget session, and the High Court had upheld his order. In this case, *State of Punjab v. Satyapal Dang* (A.I.R.1969, S.C.903) it was observed:

For those who think that the laws are defective, the path of reform is open, but in a democracy such as ours, to weaken the judiciary is to weaken democracy itself. Where the law is silent the courts have discretion. The existence of law containing its own guiding principles reduces the discretion of courts to a minimum.. The courts must do their duty according to their own understanding of the laws and the obligations of the Constitution. They cannot take their cue from sentiments of politicians nor even indirectly give support to something which they consider to be wrong or against the Constitution and the laws. The good faith of the Judges is the firm bedrock on which any system of administration securely rests and an attempt to shake the people's confidence in courts is to strike at the very root of our system of democracy. The oft-quoted anger of the Executive in the United States at the time of the New Deal and the threat to the Supreme Court (which the United States had the good sense not to pursue) should really point the other way; and it should be noted that today the security of the United States rests upon its dependence on Constitution for nearly 200 years and that is mainly due to the Supreme Court.

In two cases, the Supreme Court corrected manifest injustice. They arose under the Advocates Act. In *O.N. Mahindroo v. Dist. Judge* (A.I.R.1971 S.C.107) the judges had to depart from an earlier view in the same case. He enjoyed deciding *K.A. Abbas v. Union of India* (1971 S.C.481) in which the Court elaborated the earlier decision on *Lady Chatterley's Lover* by laying down the law on censorship of cinematograph films. In the Election appeals, he insisted on an oral judgment immediately after the conclusion of arguments. This practice was introduced now in the Supreme Court. He felt that a judgment following the arguments creates a sense of complete confidence in the contesting politicians who can see for themselves the making of the judgment in relation to the arguments they advanced. In *Maganbhai Ishwarbhai Patel v. Union* (A.I.R.1969 S.C.783) he gave the leading judgment of the Court. The question was the cession of certain territories as a result of the Treaty of Arbitration between India and Pakistan. It was the first case of its kind in India. In *Dhulabhaiv. State of M.P* (A.I.R.S.C.78), a case which has since been followed almost universally, the Supreme Court indicated the limits of jurisdiction of Civil Courts in respect of disputes. The last case Justice Hidayatullah presided over was *Privy Purse* of the ex-Rulers of Indian States.

Thus, Justice Hidayatullah had the longest career of almost 25 years as a Judge. During this period, he was elected Bencher of Lincoln's Inn in 1967. He attended the Commonwealth Chief Justices' Conference at Port of Spain in Trinidad. He was invited to Geneva in 1968 for a meeting of the World Assembly of Judges and to deliver the Law Day Lecture on Human Rights. In 1968, he was asked to address the World Law Day at Bangkok. He also spoke on the Rule of Law as the true foundation of Peace. He was offered the degree of LL.D (*Honoris Causa*) by the University of Philippines. In Manila, he was given the 'Key' to the City of Manila. On September 12, 1968, he was invited to deliver the Eighth Feroze Gandhi Memorial Lecture. He chose *The Keynote of the Constitution* as the subject. This lecture supplemented his views in the *Golaknath* case. He heard the *Privy Purse* case and decided it in favour of the Princes. On December 6, 1969, he was invited by the Indian community in London to deliver a lecture on Guru Nanak Devji. He retired on December 17, 1970 having reached the age of 65 years. He expired on November 11, 1992.

The published work of Justice Hidayatullah includes *Democracy in India and the Judicial Process* (1966), the *South-West Africa Case* (1967) and *My Own Boswell* (Autobiography, 1970). After retirement he edited the 17th edition (1972) and 18th edition (1977) of Mulla's *Mohomedan Law* (1968). *A Judge's Miscellany* (1972) and *A Judge's Miscellany* (Second Series, 1979) followed. In 1975, he was invited by the Universities of Southern Illinois and Harvard to deliver five lectures. They have been published as *U.S.A and India.* During his spare time he advised some parties who consulted him and heard a number of important arbitration cases as the sole arbitrator. Chief among these was arbitration in a long pending dispute between the Indian Oil Corporation and Gujarat Electricity Board. Libya invited him for advice on some international problems.

In his life, Justice Hidayatullah concluded that hard work pays rich dividends and if one anticipates events and prepares in advance the labour is much less in the long run. He also learnt that opportunity does not knock twice and one must make good the first time.

9

Varahagiri Venkata Giri

Tenure as Acting President
3 May 1969-20 July 1969
Tenure as President
24 August 1969-24 August 1974
Votes Secured: 401,515
Nearest Rival
N. Sanjiva Reddy
Votes Secured: 313,548

1894-1980

Varahagiri Venkata Giri, apart from being the fourth President of India, attained eminence in public life by the strength of his character and a spirit of independence. Unlike most leaders of India's freedom struggle who were helped in their careers by the bounty of both nature and circumstance, Giri lacked all the ready vehicles to greatness. Physically with robust frame, though both commanding and lovable, but not exactly the photographer's delight, with rotund figure that robs the personality of elegance to attract the audience, Giri's heavy-lidded eyes peering out of a tough bald skull spoke of the man of action. Starting his political career not as an idol of the masses or as a romantic revolutionary but as a trade unionist at a time when trade unionism was not the vogue among the public, he rose to pinnacle by virtues of the qualities, which he displayed.

Giri was born on August 10, 1894, and was the second child of the family of 12—seven boys and five girls.

He was born and brought up in the primarily agricultural hinterland on the East Coast, the veritable backwaters of political India. He was the son of Jogaiah Pantulu, a practicing lawyer at Berhampur. The Neogi sub-caste among Andhra Brahmins, of whom Giri was one, is known for its flair for diplomacy and sophistication. Giri's grandfather, Ramaiah Pantulu, was the first in the Giri family to study English. He won a gold medal by standing first in the Intermediate Examination of Madras University in 1860. He had his own practice as a first-grade *vakil* and became an undisputed leader of the Bar at Ganjam and was appointed Pleader and Public Prosecutor. Giri's mother played a vital role in shaping his character. She was perhaps one of the very few women to have the benefit of education in those days. The result was that she was able to combine the mother's instinct with an intelligent woman's understanding of worldly problems in rearing children. During the freedom struggle, when four of her surviving children, including Giri, went to jail, and her own husband was in the thick of the non-cooperation movement, renouncing the life of comfort they were used to, she not only put up with it stoically but was a pillar of strength to the movement. She would never let despair and demoralization overtake the household.

Giri's was a kind of a 'socialist' joint family. The children were allowed full freedom to express their views on many matters. Their lapses were brought home to them without admonition or punishment. Such an upbringing had the double advantage of making the boy self-confident and teaching him to respect a different viewpoint. His uncle, D. Hanumantha Rao, who practiced the precept of 'service above self', also influenced the boy. He would attend the sick and nurse the ailing in the family as well as in the town. As a teenager, Giri would follow with interest and admiration his father's speeches at the district and provincial political conferences. Giri's father was an important member of the pre-Gandhian Indian National Congress and attended many of his annual conferences. The eloquence of the great leaders and the rhetoric of their pronouncements fascinated the boy. He would jot down their speeches and incorporate large chunks from them into his own essays and speeches, irrespective of their relevance to the topics under discussion. He mesmerized his audience with the words of learned length and thundering sound when he participated in the debates.

When Giri was 13, his elder brother, who was his senior by three years, died. It made Giri the *de facto* eldest son and prop of the family. After passing the Senior Cambridge Examination in Madras (now, Chennai), Giri set sail for the United Kingdom to qualify himself for the bar. One of his mother's injunctions on the eve of his departure was that he should remain a strict vegetarian when abroad. It became such an obsession with young Giri that he would repeatedly make sure from the ship's bearers that a dish was vegetarian before partaking of it. Table manners proved another problem. Until then, Giri had not handled a fork or knife. But he would not give himself away so easily. On the first night, on the boat, he feigned lack of appetite and contented himself with a cup of coffee at the dinner table, while watching how the others ate. He got over the nervousness on the following day and managed to use knife and fork. In Ireland, he took a fancy for the National University of Ireland and the Kings Inn, Dublin, where he studied to become a barrister. For a *Brahmin* youth reared in orthodox practices and rituals, it was a novel experience to sail to England aboard a westernized P & O Liner. He reached Colombo via Dhanushkodi and boarded a ship for London.

For a youth unused to the ways of Western civilization congenial company was naturally necessary under an alien sky. Therefore, when he decided to go to Ireland for his higher education, he was not so much prompted by the affinity between the Indian freedom struggle and the Irish urge for self-government as by the fact that there were many Andhra students studying there at that time. For his B,A degree he took literature, economics, political science, constitutional law and international law. Unlike in England, where there was then an undercurrent of racial and colour prejudice against Indian students, there were no such disabilities in Ireland. The Irish treated Indians as equals and would not let religious differences or disparity in customs and ways of living to colour their attitude. His stay in Ireland enabled him to develop contacts with Irish leaders. Ireland then was in the throes of a political upheaval and social revolution. The Irish extremist movement for Independence excited Giri, but the abortive Easter rebellion brought home to him the perils of ill-planned violent agitation. He joined the Irish Anarchical Society with a view to use the experience and knowledge gained from the Irish struggle to wage a violent agitation against the British in India.

Giri's first contact with Mahatma Gandhi was in London. Giri was there to spend the summer vacation in the British capital. Mahatma Gandhi did not, in those days, approve of the youngsters' opposition to British dress. The Mahatma himself would sport a suit, complete with a bowler hat. He advised Giri that there was nothing wrong in dressing like an Englishman while in England. But Giri would not heed the elder's word. He stuck to his fez cap, which landed him in trouble in 1915. He was on a visit to the Port of Cork in southern Ireland where British warships were berthed. Taking Giri to be a Turk (Turkey was an enemy country then) the police took him into custody on account of the cap he was wearing. Giri was left free only when he told the police that he was an Indian student of Dublin University and was on a sightseeing trip to Cork. The Easter rebellion of 1916 and its unpleasant aftermath made a deep impression on Giri's mind. He vowed to put into practice in India what he had seen and learnt in Ireland. The strike by the dockers, coal-miners, railwaymen and transport workers, which preceded the revolt, stirred him deeply and brought home to him the efficacy of organized working class action. He gave up the idea of pursuing his studies either in England or in the USA and started the return voyage.

Giri's experiences in Ireland created in him an urge to strive for the country's freedom. Politics at that time was not the asylum of all those who had either failed in other walks of life or lacked the mental and other equipment to make headway elsewhere. It was the chosen career of men and women who were inspired by lofty ideals and were prepared to suffer and sacrifice for them. In India, Giri met Prakasham, who became his political guru, and who moved Giri's enrolment as an advocate in the High Court of Madras on September 13, 1916. Giri was offered the appointment of a *munsiff*. But he declined the offer and told Prakasam of his vow as a member of the Anarchist Society in Dublin not to take up Government service until India was free of British rule. Giri now set up practice at Berhampur along with his father. As a young lawyer, Giri handled cases in the company of or in opposition to such luminaries as Sir S.P. Sinha, Sir B.C. Mitter, N.N, Sankar, Srinivasa Iyengar and S. Varadchari. But he gave up practice hardly after five years and plunged into the freedom movement. In 1916, he became a formal member of the Indian National Congress.

Giri attended the Lucknow Congress in 1916. For him, the metamorphosis in the thinking and approach of the Congress was extremely welcome. He and his friends enthusiastically joined the *satyagraha* movement launched by Mahatma Gandhi in 1921. It took the form of contravention of the excise regulations by picketing liquor shops. Giri, along with 350 others, offered *satyagraha* in Ganjam and was arrested. His first taste of jail life began in February 1922. Jail life provided him an opportunity to win political friends and influence less initiated people. There he also led a hunger strike against unwholesome food being supplied to the prisoners and won for the *satyagrahis* the right to cook their own food with rations provided by the authorities. Spices, including salt, without which no Andhra meal could be complete, were conspicuous by their absence. So was buttermilk. After three days of hunger strike, the authorities gave in and let the political prisoners cook their own food. The criminals or non-political prisoners, who shared the jails with the *satyagrahis,* also benefited from the innovation. Giri also fought against corruption in the administration of jails.

When out of jail, Giri was approached by a group of railwaymen from Kharagpur for organizing a trade union there. He readily agreed. Thus was laid the foundation of the B.N. Railwaymen's Union, which grew into a mighty working class movement within a decade. A staunch believer in collective bargaining, Giri always regarded strikes as avoidable. He insisted that strikes should be duly given notice of and should be properly and systematically organized. His concern for workers, who lost wages by work stoppages, was even greater than that of the victims themselves. For about six months earlier, the agent of the B.N. Railway Co. played hide and seeks with the union. The tactics of the management naturally upset the workers. The strike became inevitable. Giri laid great stress on the striking workers remaining perfectly peaceful. Sabotage was an anathema to him. He never allowed workers to indulge in destructive activities as part of a strike. Giri secured the cooperation of traders, merchants and others for the striking workers to see that they do not suffer. The strike was ultimately called off in the middle of March following assurances by the management that there would be no more dismissals and that an inquiry would be held into the earlier ones.

Giri was also the President of employees' unions of Madras and Southern Mahratta Railway, the Nizam State Railway and the Mysore State Railway. He insisted the government to fix minimum wage for the workers. One of the charms of Giri had been his aversion for extremism in speech. He was never so flamboyant as to induce action, which went against the grain of his thinking. One of the leaders of the Nizam State Railway Union had issued circular exhorting workers to indulge in violence. The management got hold of a copy of the circular and confronted Giri with this. The management threatened to cancel the recognition of the union on the ground that one of its office-bearers had instigated workers to violence. Giri owned responsibility for the circular. The ring of sincerity Giri had brought to bear on it carried the day. Similarly, he led some more strike but he was always found reasonable.

In the year 1935, by the time Giri was forty he was elected to the Central Legislative Assembly. His ideal had been the welfare State. As Labour Minister of Madras, during 1937-39, he tried to live up to the Congress labour policy, as laid down in the election manifesto. One of his first acts as minister was to formulate a labour policy and announce it.The accent on collective bargaining was the crux of Giri's approach to labour disputes. It consisted of securing for the workers "a decent standard of living, reasonable hours of work and conditions of labour in conformity, as far as economic conditions of the country permitted, with international standards, suitable machinery for settlement of disputes between employers and workmen, protection against the economic consequences of old age, sickness and unemployment and the right of workers to form unions and to strike for the protection of their interests. No Socialist or Communist could offer more. But Giri never had a fascination for doctrines which, according to him, almost always degenerated into dogmas. Being extremely ethical-minded he was also repelled by the materialist bias of scientific socialism. An intense nationalist, he had no patience with those who put too much emphasis on the international experience of the working class. Even as a trade unionist, Giri was prompted by his nationalist urge. When the workers of Coimbatore textile mills struck work following a wage dispute, prompt appointment of a court of inquiry eased the situation and the strike was called off.

After a brief spell of 30 months as Labour Minister in the Union Government, Giri resigned on August 30, 1954 over a majority decision of the Nehru Cabinet to amend an award given by the Industrial Appellate Tribunal in disputes between the different banks and their employees. Giri had never been a protagonist of adjudication. He had all along stood for collective bargaining between workers and their employers, a principle which it had been accepted all round would have obviated the complex situation created by the Bank Award. When the Appellate Tribunal gave its award in the bank dispute the majority opinion in the Government was that it needed modification "in the larger interests of the community". Giri could not stomach this.

In 1950, Giri tried to bring about a rapprochement between the Congress-controlled Indian National Trade Union Congress and the Socialist Hind Mazdoor Sabha. He thought that there was not much difference between them, except in tactics. Therefore, even before he became Labour Minister he tried for a merger of the two. He was extremely happy when two rival federations of railwaymen merged (though temporarily) and three organizations of civilian defence personnel came together. He felt that such restrictions created 'artificial peace', leading to a 'cease-fire atmosphere'. Instead of producing healthy labour-management relations, they generated bitterness among the parties. Moreover, notwithstanding the law, there had been 'illegal strikes', putting the Government in an embarrassing position because it could not put down mass action, at least not for long. He felt that an agreement arrived at after negotiation would always be more conscientiously observed and regarded as more binding by both parties than any statutory regulation, for the enforcement of which a cumbersome legal procedure has to be adopted. At the same time, he laid down stress on preventive measures.

From 1957 to 1967 Giri was the Governor of the States of Uttar Pradesh, Kerala and Mysore. Keeping aloof from active politics of a controversial nature, he helped the States to tide over many complicated situations. How could a stormy petrel be a ceremonial figurehead? He was just past sixty. He was not cut out for the politics, which was in vogue. As a Congressman, he belonged to the generation, which was straightforward in its dealings. As a trade unionist, he put principles above party interests. The 'currents' at play in Uttar Pradesh were primarily the product of internecine rivalry inside the ruling Congress Party. The Opposition groups were too weak and were divided to take political advantage of the growing chaos inside the governing party. Therefore, the healing touch required of a Governor like Giri who could sort out the group differences. It was, no doubt, a delicate task. Soon he took over as Governor of Kerala. Giri told a meeting of the Industrial Relations Board in December 1960 that it was the duty of all well wishers of Kerala to dispel the impression of insecurity in the State. The Chief Minister realized the importance of attracting capital to Kerala and even took steps in that direction.

As Vice-President, Giri chaired the Rajya Sabha proceedings. He was not new to Parliament, having made a mark both in the Central and Provincial legislatures. He was intensely conscious of the potentialities of the parliamentary system. He was visibly elated when an M.P effectively used the forum of Parliament to elicit information, keep the Government on its toes thus maintaining a check on the Executive. He was happy when the angularities of official policies were rounded out by the interplay of opinions. But misuse of the opportunities for mounting political propaganda or indulging in personal vilification of political opponents dismayed him. He disliked being put in the position of a schoolteacher while regulating the business of mature assembly of lawmakers.

When Dr Zakir Husain passed away, while in office, he felt that as had been the convention the Presidency should automatically be passed on to him. When the Congress Parliamentary Party nominated Neelam Sanjiva Reddy, he resisted and contested the Presidential election as an independent candidate. In a statement seeking the support of the voters, he wrote: "The Head of the State is a symbol of the unity of the nation and, therefore, it is necessary that the office of the President should be kept above party-considerations. I am an Indian first, last and always before I belong to this party or that party, this group or that group, I stand for the fundamental right adumberated in the Constitution of India, especially the right to work and the right to live and for other amenities which will make the common man's life reasonably happy." Giri's sincerity, it seems, won him support from progressive-minded people all over the country.

After assuming office as President of India in August 1969, he said: "I am only a common man having spent the major part of my life as an active participant in the working class movement and in the service of the under-privileged sections of our society. By instinct and training, therefore, I am first and foremost a servant of the people." As President of India, he shared with the Prime Minister of India an ardent urge to fight poverty and backwardness. Significantly, one of Giri's first acts as President of India in 1969 was to give assent to the nationalization of banks. Both the Prime Minister and the President had the same perception. Like Indira Gandhi, he believed in planned development of national resources, radical land reforms and speedy elimination of social and economic disparities. He was also deeply committed to the parliamentary system and fundamental human freedom. He was immune from the caste or religious loyalties or bigotry.

With his abiding love for the people and their welfare he fully supported the programmes of Prime Minister Indira Gandhi. He addressed Indira Gandhi as "daughter". In order to silence his critics he openly admitted that as a Constitutional Head of the State he had to act on the advice of the Prime Minister. President V.V. Giri's tenure ended on August 24, 1974 and a 25 paise stamp was issued in his honour when he laid down office as the President of India. He was awarded Bharat Ratna in 1975 for his long service to the nation.

On June 24, 1980, at the age of 65, Giri had a massive heart attack at his residence in Madras (now, Chennai) and he breathed his last. He left behind four sons and seven daughters. His wife, Saraswati, had already expired two years earlier. He had expressed a wish that he be given a simple funeral. Accordingly, the family utilized the money for feeding the poor instead of spending it on rituals. He was cremated in the crematorium where Dr S. Radhakrishnan was cremated six years back. A week before his death, he wrote an open letter to the then Prime Minister urging her to convene a second Constituent Assembly to have a fresh look at the Constitution in view of the changed situations and also suggested her the formation of a national government under her leadership to overcome the immediate problems.

V.V. Giri was the author of *Industrial Relations, Labour Problems in Indian Jobs for Our Millions Industry,* and *My Life and Times*. He was awarded D. Litt (*Honoris Causa*) by Banaras Hindu University, Andhra University and Lucknow University. Agra, Moscow, Bulgaria and Bratislava universities conferred on him LL. D for his distinguished contributions. Above all, V.V. Giri's personal qualities are the key to his eminence. There had been many crucial moments and it was on such occasions that his inner moral fibre was severally tested. In the broadest sense, Giri's greatness was on account of his role as an effective link among diverse forces at work in the Indian society. He was a good man by any reckoning.

10

Fakhruddin Ali Ahmed

Tenure as President
24 August 1974-11 Feb 1977
Votes Secured: 754,113
Nearest Rival
Tridib Chaudhuri
Votes Secured: 189,196

1905-1977

Fakhruddin Ali Ahmed had been the fifth President of India who adorned Rashtrapati Bhavan from 1974 to 1977. Before him, V.V. Giri was the acting President during May-July 1969 and Justice Hidayatullah acted from July to August 1969. He succeeded V.V. Giri who was the President of India again from 1969 to 1974. He was, in fact, the second President from the minority community and was the choice of the Congress Party.

Born on May 13, 1905 at Hauz Qazi area of old Delhi with a silver spoon in his mouth, Fakhruddin Ali Ahmed was one of those few Muslims who, by virtue of his service to the country under the leadership of Mahatma Gandhi, reached the pinnacle of honour as the President of the Indian Republic. His grandfather, Khaliluddin Ali Ahmed, married in one of the families who were the relics of Emperor Aurangzeb's bid to conquer Assam. His father, Col. Zalnur Ali, of the Indian Medical Service, had to leave Assam while he was a bachelor doctor following an incident in Shillong, where he married the daughter of the Nawab of Lohari in Delhi. Fakhruddin was born here. He was the fourth child of Zalnur Ali Ahmed's five sons and five daughters. Fakhruddin's father was a staunch nationalist and this obviously had a great impact on the young boy.

Fakhruddin was first educated in the Bonda Government High School in Uttar Pradesh in northern India. He matriculated from the Delhi Government High School, then under the Punjab University. He was sent to England for higher education in 1923 and to prepare for the I.C.S, though his mother was opposed to his son being sent abroad. He joined the Catherine College of Cambridge University and was called to the Bar from Inner Temple of London. He could not compete for the I.C.S examination due to illness. On return to India he started legal practice in the Lahore High Court in 1928. In October that year, his father, accompanied by his Barrister son, Fakhruddin, paid a visit to Guwahati to look after his paternal property which included a few hundred acres of land in and around Guwahati, and thus the family's link, snapped on Col. Zalnur Ali's posting outside Assam, was re-established. Here, Fakhruddin came in contact with the leaders of the Congress in Assam and in 1931 enrolled himself as its primary member.

During his stay in England, Fakhruddin met Jawaharlal Nehru in 1925 whose progressive ideas impressed and influenced him considerably. On return to India, he actively participated in the freedom movement. He offered himself for *satyagraha* on December 14, 1940 and he was incarcerated for a year. Again, in the Quit India Movement he was arrested on August 9, 1942 and was detained as a security prisoner for three and a half years. He was released in April 1945. He was elected to the Assam Assembly for the first time in 1935 and became the Minister of Finance, Revenue and Labour in the Congress Coalition Ministry formed by the late Gopinath Bardolol on September 19, 1938. As a Minister, he demonstrated his acumen and ability in administrative sphere. He initiated the Assam Agricultural Income Tax Bill that levied taxes on tea garden lands in the Province. It was a bold measure.

On November 9, 1945, at the age of 40, Fakhruddin married 21-years old Abida Hyder, the daughter of Mohammed Sultan Hyder "Josh", a member of the Civil Service. When negotiations for the wedding were underway, Fakhruddin was undergoing a jail term in Jorhat as security prisoner. At a certain stage of the negotiations Abida's family wanted to know what the prospective bridegroom was doing. The answer came from one of the relatives of the would-be bridegroom: *fil hal to jail mein hai* (at present, he is in jail). But the destiny still brought Fakhruddin and Abida into wedlock. Abida had graduated from the Aligarh Muslim University. The couple was blessed with three children—first a son, Parveze, next a daughter, Semina, and the youngest child, a son, Badar Durrez. Begum Abida was elected to the Lok Sabha from Bareilly Parliamentary Constituency on Congress (I) ticket in a bye-election in June 1981. She was once again elected to the Lok Sabha from the same constituency in the 1984 Lok Sabha election.

When the Congress Ministry, headed by Gopinath Bardolo, was formed in Assam on February 11, 1946, Fakhruddin Ali Ahmed became the Advocate-General of Assam and worked in this capacity till 1952 when he was elected to the Rajya Sabha. In 1955, he led a delegation of Indian Lawyers to the USSR. In 1957, he was a member of Assam Legislative Assembly with a thumping majority and became Minister for Finance, Law, Community Development, Panchayati Raj and Local-self Government. In 1962, he was re-elected to the Assam Legislative Assembly and was once again included in the Council of Ministers with the same portfolios. In 1964, he visited the USA on an official invitation and on his way back home he visited Japan and Hong Kong. In 1965, he represented the Government of India at the Independence Day celebrations of Malaysia and the inauguration of international mosque and airport at Kuala Lumpur. In 1966, he took over as the Secretary of All India Ghalib Centenary Celebrations Committee from Dr Zakir Husain. As Committee's Secretary, he was also instrumental in the building of a Ghalib complex, comprising of an auditorium, a museum and a research library near the Irwin Hospital in New Delhi. Ghalib Auditorium was inaugurated on August 23, 1973 by the then Prime Minister Indira Gandhi.

Though Fakhruddin Ali Ahmed occupied a senior position in the Chaliha Ministry from 1957 he was asked by Jawaharlal Nehru to join his Cabinet at the Centre in January 1966. He was elected to the Lok Sabha from the Barpeta constituency in 1971. In the Central Cabinet he was given the important portfolios relating to Food and Agriculture, Cooperation, Education, Industrial Development and Company Law. His induction to the Central Cabinet was perhaps because of his close link with, and loyalty to the Nehru family and also for his acumen in administration. As Union Cabinet Minister, Fakhruddin Ali Ahmed visited the U.K., West Germany, Bulgaria, Hungary, France, Italy, USSR, Sri Lanka and Iran. In September 1969, he represented the Government of India at the Islamic Conference at Rabat in Morocco. In September 1970, he attended FAO's Conference in Australia as a special guest and visited Japan, Hong Kong and Philippines. In 1971, he visited the Arab countries as a special emissary of the Government of India to present the Government's point of view on military action taken by Pakistan in the then East Pakistan. In November 1971 and November 1973, he was a member of the Indian delegation to the FAO Council's Session in Rome. As a Union Minister he also remained as the Chairman of the Central Wakf Council.

In the Congress Party, Fakhruddin Ali Ahmed enjoyed an enviable position. He had been a member of the Congress Working Committee for several years. When the Congress Party was split in 1969, Fakhruddin Ali Ahmed remained with Indira Gandhi, may be because of his deep-rooted association with the Nehru family. Again, Because of his allegiance to the Congress Party and the Nehru family he was nominated to the highest post of the land – the presidentship of the Indian Republic. He was declared elected in a direct contest with Tridib Choudhury, a nominee of eight opposition parties, securing more than 80 per cent of the votes polled, though the Congress had a two-third majority in the Electoral College comprising of the elected members of Parliament and State Assemblies. He resigned as Speaker of the Lok Sabha and on August 24, 1974, he was sworn in as the fifth President of India.

In 1975, President Fakhruddin Ali Ahmed represented the Government of India at the funeral of King Faisal of Saudi Arabia. Later, he visited a number of Muslim countries like Indonesia, Egypt, Sudan, Iran, United Arab Emirates, Malaysia and Saudi Arabia. He also visited Hungary and Yugoslavia. He was keen on getting Urdu its rightful place and clarified that no language could prosper with state patronage and that for its development it is essential to have its roots in the masses. He advised the people not to resort to agitation to make their language popular. Rather, he warned that such a step can be detrimental to the cause of its development. He also asked the Muslims not to link Urdu and Muslims, as Urdu is not the language of Muslims alone. He reminded the Muslims that all Muslims, spread over the world, do not speak one language. He was also averse to the imposition of any language on a section of the people.

On February 6, 1997, President Fakhruddin Ali Ahmed left for a State visit to Malaysia, Philippines and Burma. While in Kuala Lumpur he felt indisposed and had to return back to India. On February 11, 1977, he collapsed in his bathroom at 8 a.m. He was laid to eternal rest on February 13, 1997 with full State honours beside the green-domed Jama Masjid in Parliament Street, New Delhi. He had special attachment with this place and used to offer his Friday prayers at this place. It is just a matter of coincidence that the day he expired also happened to be Friday. He will be remembered as a staunch nationalist and an illustrious statesman who symbolized the best traditions of India's composite culture.

Suave and sober, Fakhruddin Ali Ahmed seldom allowed anger and prejudices to get better of him. At the same time, he did not compromise with unprincipled issues. These traits of his character were apparently the key to his success in his public life and endeared him to all sections of the masses. Towards the end of his political career he was, however, accused of being communal by some people, but it can be proved baseless if we know his background. He had always been loyal to the Congress Party and tried to bring to its fold a number of Aligarh Muslim University educated youths of his community whose communal outlook was a public knowledge. He had an unflinching love for the country and his faith in secularism was profound..

Though politics was Fakhruddin Ali Ahmed's forte, his deep interest in sports and other extra-mural activities was well-known. He was a tennis player and golfer and was elected President of the Assam Football Association and the Assam Cricket Association for several terms. He was also the Vice President of the Assam Sports Council. In April 1967, he was elected President of the All India Cricket Association besides being a member of the Delhi Golf Club and the Delhi Gymkhana Club since 1961. His love for music and finer arts was immense. He was deeply interested in poetical works of Ghalib. His travels to the USSR, the USA, the UK, Japan, Malaysia and many Arab countries as a Minister and afterwards as the President of India widened his urbane outlook that endeared him to all sections of the people, irrespective of caste, creed and a vocation. Elegantly dressed he was always courteous but firm in what he considered to be just and fair and presented himself as a Moghul.

In the final analysis, Fakhruddin Ali Ahmed was a great freedom fighter, a sportsman, a successful Advocate and a man of very modest habits. He neither smoked nor even consumed *paan* (betel-leaf). He was invariably meticulously and elegantly dressed. He was then the only Indian President who occasionally wore western dress. The game of golf was his regular feature. With a fine sense of humour, Fakhruddin Ali Ahmed was equally fond of light and classical music. Like V.V. Giri, he will also be remembered for maintaining cordial relations with Prime Minister Indira Gandhi during his presidency even when the need was to assert himself or to render his advice. President Fakhruddin Ali Ahmed and Prime Minister Indira Gandhi attended each other's family ceremonies like betrothals and weddings. Prime Minister's grand children, Rahul and Priyanka, participated in the birthday parties of President's grand children, Samir and Taleya. Prime Minister Indira Gandhi always visited the President to felicitate him on the occasion of *Id*. The President and the First Lady, Begum Abida Ahmed, used to visit the Prime Minister on her birthdays. President's assent to the proclamation of Emergency without any hesitation was, perhaps, the only controversial instance during his tenure.

The Government of the State of Assam has instituted Fakhruddin Ali Ahmed Memorial Award for National Integration. While presenting this award on February 18, 2011, Prime Minister Manmohan Singh said that this award is a small token of our gratitude to one of the great sons of Assam and India. Fakhruddin Ali Ahmed's contribution to the Indian freedom struggle was invaluable. A firm believer in the ideals of Mahatma Gandhi and Jawaharlal Nehru, he left an indelible imprint on the political landscape of our great nation. Fakhruddin Ali Ahmed's long and distinguished career in public life, which culminated in his occupying the august position of President of India, is a shining example of commitment to ethical values and selfless service to the people. Indeed, his contribution to the building of our society and country continues to inspire all of us, said Prime Minister Dr Manmohan Singh.

11

Basappa Danappa Jatti

Tenure as Acting President
11 Feb. 1977-25 July 1977

1912-2002

Basappa Danappa Jatti, the soft-spoken Acting President of India, was born on September 7, 1912 in a Kannada Lingayat family at Savalgi in Jamakhandi Taluk of Bijapur district in Karnataka state. He rose from a humble beginning as a Municipality member to India's second-highest office during a five-decade-long chequered political career. He was Acting President of India from February 11, 1977 to July 25, 1977.

After completing his graduation in law from Sykes Law College, Kolhapur, when it was affiliated with the then University of Bombay, B. D. Jatti did his legal practice as an advocate for a very short span of time in his home town Jamakhandi. In 1940, he entered in politics as a Municipality member at Jamakhandi and was finally elected as a member of the Jamakhandi State Legislature.

Jatti practiced for a brief period as a pleader in Jamakhandi. He was appointed minister of Jamakhandi state. On March 8, 1948 after Jamakhandi was merged with Bombay state, he returned to legal practice and continued it for 20 months. Jatti was also nominated as member of the Bombay State Legislative Assembly to represent the merged area, and, within a week of his nomination, he was appointed

Parliamentary Secretary to the then Bombay Chief Minister, B.G Kher. He worked in that capacity for a couple of years. After serving for two years as the Private Secretary to the Bombay Chief Minister, Jatti was appointed Deputy Minister for Health and Labour. After that he was appointed as the Chairman of Land Reforms Committee in the Mysore Legislative Assembly.

After the 1952 general election, he was appointed Minister of Health and Labour in the then Bombay Government and held that post till the reorganisation of states. Jatti became member of the Mysore Legislative Assembly after the reorganisation and was Chairman of the Land Reforms Committee. He became Chief Minister in 1958 and continued in that office until 1962.

In the third general election in 1962, he was re-elected from Jamkhandi constituency and appointed as Finance Minister in the Nijalingappa Ministry. He was re-elected from Jamkhandi constituency in the third general election and was appointed Finance Minister on July 2, 1962 in the Nijalingappa Ministry. He was re-elected to the fourth Assembly from the same constituency and was appointed as Minister of Food and Civil Supplies.

Jatti subsequently moved onto the national scene and was appointed Lt. Governor of Pondicherry (now, Puducherry) in 1968. He became Governor of Orissa in 1973 and, in 1974, assumed office as the fifth Vice-President until 1980. He was also the ex-officio Chairman, Rajya Sabha, till 1979.

He also held the Office of the President of India for a brief period of five months from February 11, 1977 to July 25, 1977 due to the sudden death of Fakruddin Ali Ahmed, the then President of India. He passed away on June 8, 2002.

A deeply religious man, he was also founder president of the Basava Samithi, which propagated the preachings of 12th century saint philosopher, Basaveshwara. He was also involved in various organisations concerned with social activities. Outside politics, Jatti was founder president of the Basava Samithi, a religious movement which propagated the preachings of 12th century saint, philosopher and Hindu reformer Basaveshwara.

12
Neelam Sanjiva Reddy

Tenure as President

25 July 1977-25 July 1982

Even though 37 candidates filed their nominations, 36 of them were rejected leading to Sanjiva Reddy being the only President of India till then to win unopposed.

1913-1996

Dr Neelam Sanjiva Reddy happened to be the sixth President of India, a veteran statesman and an able administrator. It is an irony of life that though, as a nominee of the Congress Parliamentary Party for presidentship, he lost the election in 1969, but later became the sixth President of India who was elected unopposed in the 1977 election. All political parties unanimously sponsored him as the consensus candidate for presidentship. He became the second non-Congress candidate to be elected as the President of India. The first one was V.V. Giri who was the non-Congress and non-official candidate, though he had the support of the Congress members led by the then Prime Minister India Gandhi, but contested the presidential election as an independent candidate. He held many eminent positions in public life both before and after independence.

Born on May 19, 1913 in a village Illur, 29 kms away from Anantapur town in Andhra Pradesh in South India, Sanjiva Reddy was the son of Neelam Chinnappa Reddy who was keen to give value-added education to his son. With this aim in view, Sanjiva Reddy was admitted in Adyar School, Madras (now, Chennai), one of the famous institutions run on the lines of Tagore's Shantiniketan where most of the young leaders shaped their careers. It was a school that nurtured free thoughts among its pupils. Sanjiva had his primary education in this school. He passed his higher education from Arts College, Anantapur. In 1931, influenced by Mahatma Gandhi, Sanjiva Reddy gave up his studies and participated in the country's freedom struggle. He was 16-years old when he met Mahatma Gandhi. When Mahatma Gandhi visited Anantapur District he was staying with his parents in Bangalore. Gandhiji used to auction the gifts and mementos received from the people. The young boy participated in Mahatma Gandhi's auction in Anantapur District and purchased a *shawl*, a casket and a painting. The same day, influenced by Gandhiji, he discarded his foreign clothes and took to *khadi* as his dress. In 1933, he resigned from his Munsif's post and became a Congress worker. He took keen interest in collecting funds for the paper, *Swaraj*. He started participating in strikes in his college at Anantapur. When the Principal of the college suspended a student for wearing a Gandhi cap on his head, all the students, under the leadership of Sanjiva Reddy, wore Gandhi caps in protest. In 1931, he left his college to serve the country. He used to say:, "I am not a college graduate but I am a graduate in life that is what my colleagues in the Movement said".

On June 8, 1935, Sanjiva Reddy married Naga Ratnamma. They had one son and three daughters. His son, Sudhir, has an independent profession and is a surgeon. He is running his own clinic in Anantapur. In 1940, Sanjiva Reddy took part in the Civil Disobedience Movement and actively participated in the activities of the Youth Congress. In 1937, at the age of 25, he became the Secretary of the Andhra Provincial Committee and continued to hold it till 1946. In 1940, he participated in the individual Satyagraha Movement and was sentenced to six months' rigorous imprisonment on December 21, 1940 or, in default, to undergo further imprisonment for six months. He was first put in Vellore jail and then in Tiruchinappali's jail. After his release he was again arrested under the Defence of India Rules and incarcerated in the Vellore jail from June 1, 1941 to March 18, 1942. Subsequently, he took an active part in the Quit India Movement and was once again taken into custody on August 11, 1942 and was imprisoned till 1945 in the Vellore and Amaravathi jails.

In 1946, Sanjiva Reddy was elected to the Madras Legislative Assembly and later became the Secretary of the Congress Legislative Party in Madras State. In the year 1947, though still quite young, he was elected a member of the Constituent Assembly of India in recognition of his services to the nation. From 1949 to April 1951 he served as Minister for Prohibition, Housing and Forests in the composite State of Madras State. In 1951, he resigned this office to contest the election for the presidentship of the Andhra Pradesh Congress Committee which he won. It was during this period that Sanjiva Reddy suffered a terrible tragedy in the death of his five year old son in a motor accident. This shocked him so deeply that he resigned the APCC presidentship. Later, however, he was prevailed upon to withdraw his resignation.

In 1952, Sanjiva Reddy was elected Member of the Rajya Sabha. In 1953, he accepted the post of Deputy Chief Minister in the Cabinet of the late Shri T Prakasam, even though he was elected the Leader of the Congress Legislature Party. He was again elected to the Legislative Assembly in 1955 and became Deputy Chief Minister in B. Gopala Reddi's Cabinet.

In 1956, when election of the leader of the United Congress Legislative Party of both Andhra and Telangana became imminent and no party from Telangana contested, Sanjiva Reddy was elected Chief Minister because of his diplomatic skill in handling men and matters. Soon after, as Chief Minister he honoured persons like Ayyadevara Kaleswara Rao, Hanumantha Rao and Gottipati Brahmaiah by offering them the posts of Speakership and Chairmanship respectively in the Assembly. Thus, by honouring the people who had contributed towards the cause of the nation he was able to win their respect. As Chief Minister, he was quite tactful in handling men and matters and never allowed himself to become the prisoner of any complexes based on considerations of false prestige by allowing prejudices and preconceived notions to blur his vision. He succeeded in winning over some of his opponents by following Buddha's injunction,: "Hatred is not eliminated by hatred but by love". Chanakya and Machiavelli virtually remained his torchbearers. He carefully studied and analyzed the problems of administration and with his commonsense and administrative acumen he successfully tackled the most exacting problem of integrating the services and administrative system of the Telangana and Andhra wings of the new State. His strategy was based on the principle of compromise and, thus, he was able to achieve uniformity in due course.

As Chief Minister, Sanjiva Reddy realized that the development of agriculture and industry was important for the prosperity of the nation. A number of schemes were initiated. When Andhra Pradesh was established there was only one Hydel Station—the Nizam Sagar—which too had yet to be commissioned. With his characteristic drive, energy and far-sighted vision he set about the task of giving Andhra Pradesh an efficient system of irrigation and electricity. Nagarjuna Sagar project was planned and the approval of the Planning Commission was secured. It turned out to be one of the largest and most prestigious masonry dams in the world, constructed across the river Krishna for irrigation and generation of power, designed to irrigate an area of two million acres of land. The project combines the cultural importance with engineering skill. The precious wealth of Buddhistic culture is preserved in the island museum in the middle of the man-made lake which presents a grand spectacle. It has become the attraction of tourists and a pilgrim centre. In the words of Prime Minister Jawaharlal Nehru, it is India's "modern temple". Similarly, Srisailam project, initiated by Sanjiva Reddy, is imbued with religious and cultural importance. It has a holy temple of Lord Malikarjuna and Goddess Bratimaramba. It is one of the ancient temples of India attracting innumerable pilgrims from far off places. It has a valley in which Sri Sankaracharya, who propounded Advaita philosophy, did penance.

During his tenure as Chief Minister of Andhra Pradesh, Sanjiva Reddy also saw to it that the work on the Tungabhadra Project High Level Canal and the Pochampad Project was speeded up and much of the work was completed far ahead of schedule. He was keen on goal-setting, target fixing and time-budgeting. In this way, after finding out solutions of ticklish problems with the neighbouring states almost 464,000 acres of land in his State was brought under irrigation. The construction of the Gosthani Reservoir in Khammam district was taken up for improving inland water transport and increasing the agricultural output in tribal areas.

Electrification of villages was taken up on a top priority basis. Andhra Pradesh became one of the first States to have successfully implemented the system of Panchayati Raj. Maulana Azad Research Institute and the Majlis Adabiyate Urdu were established. Urdu was accorded the status of a regional language and Muslims were nominated to the Legislative Council. A number of grants were initiated for Scheduled Castes and Scheduled Tribes. He introduced a proposal to make economic condition and not the mere caste or race the criterion of backwardness. The apprehensions of the people of Telangana were allayed by giving them an appropriate representation in the Cabinet, the administration, and in the statutory bodies formed in the State and in other areas as well. He was quite conscious of the fact that the people of Telangana region, for historical reasons, are quite sensitive. With a view to forestall their agitations for a separate State he introduced a number of welfare measures. All this helped him to provide a stable administration and peace in his State, leaving only few occasions for turmoil. He was determined to put an end to the exploitation of peasants by landlords by introducing a number of measures. The various Land Revenue Reforms Acts passed by his Government established the peasant's right to have a better standard of living and protection against the landlords' exploitation.

A separate Directorate of Handlooms was established to give a boost to the Handloom industry and help the workers involved in this trade. Steps were taken to introduce the cash-credit system and a pilot project was undertaken in the East Godavari District. It helped in improving the finances of the Handloom Industry and stepped up the sales promotion programme. Setting up of Andhra Pradesh Khadi and Village

Industries Board paved the way for the development of *khadi*, weaving, palm-*gur* making, soap making, road-making, leather, tanning and coir products industries. Subsequently, the Board was reconstituted to control Rural Industrial Cooperatives, numbering almost 1000 in the Andhra State. The Regional Rural Artisan Training Centres were organized in 13 districts to train the villagers. Andhra Pradesh became the largest single producer of raw-hides in India.

Training-cum-production centres were established for coir industry to train people in the extraction of coir fibre from husks and in the manufacture of coir-yarn, coir-made matting, brushes, coir-brooms and other coir products. A Coir Goods factory was also established. Various schemes were launched for the development of handicrafts. These schemes related to the organization of crafts on cooperative lines. The Government provided the managerial assistance.Handicraft emporia were set up in Hyderabad and Vijayawada for marketing the handicraft items.

Efforts were made to put the State on the industrial map of India. Although the Government of India's policy resolution had assigned small industries to the private sector, the State Government established a number of training centres in job-oriented activities like carpentry, blacksmithy, iron-foundry and the manufacture of various consumer goods, such as leather articles, chalk, bicycle spares, scientific glass apparatus, stoneware and pipes. Engineering workshops were established for providing tool room and servicing facilities. A number of industries were established. Some of them are: Andhra Paper Mill, the Gudur Ceramic Factory, the Gudur Block Glass Factory, the Government Power Alcohol Factory, the Singareni Collieries, the Nizam Sugar Factory, the Azamjahi Mills, the Allwyn Metal Works, the Hyderabad Chemicals, the Sirpur Paper Mills, the Sirsilk Rayon Mills, the Hyderabad Chemicals and Fertilizers, the Praga Tools Corporation, the Synthetic Drugs in Hyderabad and the Oil Refinery in Vizag. The Nizam Sugar Factory was taken over by the Government in 1957.

In view of his distinguished contribution to the development of Andhra Pradesh, Sri Venkatesvara University in Tirupati conferred on Sanjiva Reddy the Honorary Doctorate but he never expressed his inclination to be addressed with the prefix "Dr" and firmly rejected the proposal of his admirers to erect his statute in his life time. Following some allegations leveled against his Government in the nationalization of Bus Routes, Sanjiva Reddy resigned on moral grounds. "It is a matter of my conscience and conviction", he replied to Prime Minister Jawaharlal Nehru's letter, who asked Sanjiva Reddy to reconsider his decision to relinquish the office since the court did not indict him in any way.

On January 14, 1960, Sanjiva Reddy was elected the President of the All India Congress Committee and presided over its sessions in Bangalore, Bhavanagar and Patna. In this capacity, he manifested his characteristic blend of flexibility and firmness of purpose by asserting his own individuality and was, thus, able to win the approval and cooperation of a hetrogeneous group of people. His humility, understanding and readiness to see the point in all differing voices and abundant commonsense of equity and fair play enabled him to synthesize the conflicting viewpoints and overcome the stupendous and intricate task of the Congress President. After assuming the charge as President of the AICC, his very first difficult task was to face the mid-term elections in the troublesome State of Kerala after the dismissal of Namboodripad's Government. The Congress Government at the Centre had exploited the tidal wave of popular upsurge in Kerala to topple Namboodripad's Government. This was the beginning of a new phenomenon of Indian politics, called the toppling game and the game of destabilization. Mid-term poll became inevitable. As Congress President, he toured extensively, held discussions, addressed non-stop meetings and boosted-up the morale of the rank and file of the Congress Party.

Later, Sanjiva Reddy also played an equally important role along with K. Kamaraj in evolving the new concept of 'consensus' which made the succession to the prime ministership an easy and smooth affair which resulted in the emergence of Lal Bahadur Shastri as the second Prime Minister of India. The Prime Minister inducted Sanjiva Reddy in his

Cabinet and he, thus, held the Iron and Steel portfolio. In his new capacity, Sanjiva Reddy was instrumental for the constitution of an Anglo-American Consortium for erecting a steel plant in Visakhapatnam but due to some reasons the project could not be implemented.

When Indira Gandhi became the Prime Minister following the death of Lal Bahadur Shastri in Tashkent on January 11, 1966, Sanjiva Reddy had the portfolio of Ports, Shipping and Civil Aviation. In this capacity, he played a crucial role in exposing Dharma Teja in squandering away the public money in the Shipping Corporation and the evasion of taxes to the tune of several million rupees. He was firm in handling the strike of employees of Air India and Indian Airlines. He was the key-figure of the Syndicate Group when Indira Gandhi decided on the devaluation of the rupee on the reported pressure of the World Bank and on the advice of her "Kitchen Cabinet". In the 1967 General Election, he contested from the Hindpur Parliamentary constituency and returned once again to the national political scene. He became the Speaker of the Lok Sabha in 1967.

In 1969, Nijalingappa Group in the Congress Party wanted Sanjiva Reddy, who was Lok Sabha Speaker then, to be in the running for the office of the President. On the other side, Prime Minister Indira Gandhi had been preparing the ground for ushering in socialism and for this purpose she wanted five of the top banks of India to be nationalized or in the alternative, the bank investment and government securities to be raised by about 5 per cent, yielding about Rs.2,000 million annually for the benefit of the public sector, and a ban of foreign capital to enter fields in which technical know-how was available, etc. This was opposed by the Nijalingappa Group or Syndicate of which Sanjiva Reddy was the active member. The Syndicate felt that if Sanjiva Reddy becomes the President of India, members of Lok Sabha, under Nijalingappa's guidance will submit a memorandum to the President that the Prime Minister Indira Gandhi had lost the confidence of the House and the Congress Parliamentary Party be asked to elect another leader. On July 13, 1969, V.V. Giri, the acting President of India, announced that he would be contesting election to the office of the President of India. The Parliamentary Board had already nominated Sanjiva Reddy's name. The Syndicate even met the Prime Minister to propose Sanjiva Reddy's name, but when it came to openly supporting Reddy's candidature, she resisted despite requests from the Congress President. It was believed that she secretly sent word to V.V. Giri to contest with her support. She manipulated a situation whereby Nijalingappa sought the support of the Right-wing parties. Thus, Indira Gandhi gained the tactical advantage and announced that the Congress President Nijalingappa had talks with communal and right-wing forces which went contrary to Congress principle. She seized the opportunity of appealing to Congressmen to vote according to their conscience. She did not openly ask Congressmen not to vote for Sanjiva Reddy, but the appeal of the "conscience vote" went home for the average Congress leader, immersed in Congress culture down the decades, showed aversion to communalism and "a partiality for programmes" which benefited the "teeming millions". V.V. Giri won by a margin of 14,650 votes. Giri got 420,077 votes (50.2 per cent) against 405,427 (48.5 per cent) of Sanjiva Reddy.

In 1971, Sanjiva Reddy contested the snap Lok Sabha poll on Congress (O) ticket but lost it. Congress (O) was reduced to an insignificant party. Thereafter, he decided to retire, settled down in his home town in Anantapur and devoted most of his time to agriculture.

Sanjiva Reddy re-entered active politics on May 1, 1975 when he addressed a public meeting at Hyderabad along with Jayaprakash Narayan. In 1977, following the Emergency excesses committed by Indira Gandhi's regime and the defeat of the Congress Party in the 1977 General Election, Sanjiva Reddy won from the Nandyal Parliamentary constituency in Andhra Pradesh. He was the only non-Congress candidate who emerged victorious from Andhra Pradesh. He was unanimously elected Speaker of Lok Sabha on March 26, 1977.

In July 1977, all the political parties sponsored Sanjiva Reddy's name for Presidentship of the Republic of India. He resigned his seat in the Lok Sabha. On July 25, 1977, he was sworn in as the eighth President of India. He was the fourth

President of India from southern part of India, though Dr Zakir Husain was also born in Hyderabad. During his Presidentship, the Janata Party appointed Shah Commission to probe into the excesses committed during the Emergency period of Indira Gandhi's Government. The heterogeneous constituents of Janata Party couldn't co-exist and Prime Minister Morarji Desai had to resign, paving the way for Charan Singh to head the Government. But it is unfortunate that Charan Singh dissolved the Lok Sabha even before he could win the no-confidence motion. The General Election became inevitable and Indira Gandhi and her party returned to power in 1980.

Thus, three prime ministers were sworn in during the presidentship of Neelam Sanjiva Reddy: Morarji Desai, Charan Singh and Indira Gandhi. It goes to the credit of Sanjiva Reddy that he maintained equally cordial relations with all the prime ministers. The most notable feature of his tenure was the passage of 44th Constitutional Amendment Act. The 39th Constitutional Amendment had deprived the Supreme Court of its jurisdiction to decide disputes concerning election of the President and the Vice-President. The 44th Constitutional Amendment cancelled this amendment and restored to the Supreme Court its original jurisdiction in this respect. The 42nd Constitutional Amendment Act amended Article 74 so as to make the ministerial advice binding on the President. A new provision to Article 74(1) says that the President may require Council of Ministers to reconsider its advice to him, either generally or otherwise, and the President shall act in accordance with the advice tendered after such reconsideration. While, therefore, the President remains bound by ministerial advice he now gets a limited right to refer the matter back to the Council of Ministers for reconsideration. The Amended Act has also repealed Clause (4) of Article 132 and 213 of the Constitution which made the satisfaction of the President or the Governor to issue ordinances "final and conclusive".

After completing his tenure, Sanjiva Reddy retired on July 24, 1981 and settled down in his village in Anantapur. In an informal meeting with the Press shortly before demitting office, he candidly confessed how lonely he felt during the unprecedented crisis following the Janata Party split and Morarji Desai's resignation and how he exercised his discretionary powers and took many difficult decisions in such an emergency. On June 1, 1966, he breathed his last in Bangalore. Above all, he was a successful politician and administrator. He will particularly be remembered for his contributions as Chief Minister of Andhra Pradesh.

13

Giani Zail Singh

Tenure as President
25 July 1982-25 July 1987
Votes Secured: 754,113
Nearest Rival
Justice H.R. Khanna
Votes Secured: 282,685

1916-1994

"Zindagi ke bojh ko has kar uthana chahiye,
Rah ki dushvariyoin par muskarana chahiye..."

(Face the burdens of life with a smile and laugh away obstacles that come in your way).

These were the words of the seventh President of India, Giani Zail Singh, minutes after he was elevated to the highest post in India when he met the newsmen. Such an approach also forms the quintessence of the philosophy of his life. The first Sikh, the first Punjabi and the first person belonging to the backward classes to adorn the office of Rashtrapati Bhavan, Giani Zail Singh, always smiling, dressed in all white, symbolizing purity, was a man of humble origin but with impressive achievements. Like Abraham Lincoln, he rose to the pinnacle of glory step by step from a simple and humble agriculturist artisan family to the highest office of the country and can be remembered as the man of the masses, shifting from the mud house in a village to the Rashtrapati Bhavan as the First Citizen by dint of hard work, sacrifice, dedication, integrity, courage and determination.

It is a matter of coincidence that Giani Zail Singh, born on May 5, 1916 in Sandhwan village of the erstwhile princely State of Faridkot, now in Punjab, shared his birthday with Karl Marx, the father of socialism. Zail Singh also believed in socialism. His father, Kishan Singh, belonged to an artisan family. His mother, Indi Kaur, expired when the boy was only nine-months old. His aunt, who was childless, brought up the boy as her own progeny with all the love and affection she could bestow. His father was a deeply religious man who extensively studied the Sikh traditional history and offered his daily prayers in a room where the Holy Book, *Guru Granth Sahib*, was kept. Zail Singh was the fourth and the youngest child in the family.

Zail Singh was sent to school in his village at the age of five, where he started learning Urdu and he learnt Punjabi at home. His father initiated him in the study of scriptures. He was quite young when his father taught him the recitation of the holy Sikh scripture, *Guru Granth Sahib*. At the age of seven, he could recite it with considerable ease and accuracy. He used to listen to *kirtan* recitation of holy hymns and he took to playing on the harmonium and performed perfect *shabad kirtan* with correct pronunciation. While as a young boy, he was involved with an Akali *Jatha*. Zail Singh studied up to middle class in an Urdu-medium school at Kothapura but in 1930 his father withdrew him from there and trained him to preach the ideals of Sikh *Gurus*.

At a very young age, Zail Singh developed contacts with some revolutionaries and he read two books, *Ghadar Dian Goonjan* (Echoes of Revolution) in Punjabi and *Khoon-e-Shahidan* (Blood of the Martyrs) in Urdu. The news of the execution of Bhagat Singh, Sukhdev Singh and Rajguru in the Lahore Central Jail kindled the patriotic sentiments in him. He was impressed with the devotion of the revolutionaries and was convinced that without national independence, no religion could be essentially free. He felt that slavery was a curse and it was the sacred duty of every Indian to cast away the yoke of foreign subjugation. He was now less inclined to attend religious congregations and more keen to listen to the views of political activities in their meetings.The intrepidation of the pioneers of the *Ghaddar* movement and the daring deeds of Bhagat Singh left an indelible impression on his mind. His participation in the Akali religious congregations strengthened his resolve to launch himself on the turbulent waters of the national struggle.

In 1933, for the first time, Zail Singh was arrested by the British while taking part in a march demanding democratic rights. He was incarcerated in the Lahore Central Jail. In the Jail, he had to work on ropes which made his hands "raw and bleed". Once he tore a piece of his own turban and wrapped it on his lacerated hands to do the labour. He was asked to grind 16 kilograms of wheat every day. One fine morning, he was yoked to an oil mill like a bullock to extract oil from the seeds. He made *durries, khes, khad*i cloth and even silken cloth while in jail and spent the night in the cage in utter darkness. Pen, pencil and paper were out of his reach. To acquire a pencil was a herculean task. However, if and when he could get it, he buried it under the roots of a shrub at some distance from his cell. He would dig it out at an opportune time to jot down a few lines addressed to a relative or a friend. He was put in fetters and the attrition of the iron caused a wound on his ankle, and once he started running high temperature. He used pages of the books issued to him for writing letters which were sent out in surreptitious manner. While in jail, he had an opportunity to read a number of religious books, including *Quran*. After four years in jail, he started having low-grade fever. He sought permission to visit *Gurudwara* in jail once a month. On the first day, he scooped the dust of the feet of the congregation and applied it to his body and miraculously felt relief. Thus, he completed his five years.

Zail Singh was engaged to Bibi Pradhan Kaur in 1921 when he was around 5 and Pradhan Kaur was just two years old—an age when one hardly understands as to what betrothal and marriage mean. Zail Singh resisted against marriage and went underground so that it could be postponed as he wanted to avoid it for some more time. Ultimately, he agreed, but reluctantly, as he could not displease his mother whom he considered no less than the Goddess. Finally, he was married to Pradhan Kaur on August 6, 1934 at the tender age of eighteen. Later, they had a son and three daughters.

Arya Samaj became very active in Punjab and its *Parcharaks* preached the teachings of Swami Dayanand Saraswati in public meetings organized for the purpose. In 1932, a meeting was organized at Faridkot where speakers from different religions were to address the audience on "Why I Love My Religion"? When it was found that there is no speaker to represent the Sikh view-point, Zail Singh's name was proposed. His arguments swayed all those who attended the huge gathering. He told the audience that equality, brotherhood and equality of all in the eyes of God were preached by Guru Nanak Devji some 450 years back and caste had no place in Sikhism which recognizes all the human race the world over as one. When he concluded, people carried him on their shoulders which enhanced his prestige. With great humility he attributed this honour and praise to the grace of God since, he felt, it was ordained by Him otherwise he himself was nothing.

In 1937, Zail Singh was appointed General Secretary of Faridkot Akali Dal. He felt convinced that nothing could be achieved through appeal and therefore took the path of agitations to get the grievances of the people redressed. He was against one man rule and had faith in the democratic traditions. The rulers of princely states had their own laws and regulations. They could put any person behind the bars without trial in the court of law. In a big Akali Dal congregation held on September 12, 1937 at Surgapuri, Kothapura, Zail Singh made a forceful one-hour long speech and impressed the audience by his oratory. He advised the Akali workers to join the Congress Party to get their grievances against the ruler redressed. The Akali workers liked the suggestion and joined the Congress. In Punjab, both these organizations maintained separate existence but fought together against the British imperialism and the autocrat rulers of the States in Punjab.

In 1946, Giani Zail Singh came in contact with Jawaharlal Nehru. When Nehru talked of socialism, liberty, equality and progress, Giani Zail Singh thought that he should work hard for these ideals. India became free on August 15, 1947, but the princely states were still under the yoke of feudal rulers. The efforts of the State Praja Mandal to get the grievances of the people redressed and establish people's government had failed. He then took the lead to overthrow the autocratic rule of the *Raja*. On March 1, 1948, the Faridkot Secretariat, Police Stations, State Treasuries and Courts were captured and surrounded by the volunteers. Giani Zail Singh announced the formation of a parallel government. Though this made him a hero of the people but he was prosecuted, convicted and awarded one year's rigorous imprisonment with a fine of Rs.50. The *Raja* took it as a revolt against his kingdom and in order to teach a lesson to Giani Zail Singh and the people of the State, tied his hand and foot, and tied his hair by a rope behind a jeep. He was ordered to be dragged along the streets of Faridkot. When dragged a little, wisdom dawned upon the police officers who untied him. It appeared to be a threat. He was released on March 20, 1948.

Giani Zail Singh did a marvelous service to the country and the Congress as founder of the Faridkot State Congress in 1938 and President of the Faridkot State Praja Mandal during 1946-48. On July 5, 1948, under the Union of States, Faridkot became a part of PEPSU (Punjab and East Punjab States Union). In PEPSU of independent India, he was a Cabinet minister twice. In January 20, 1949 to November 18, 1950 he was Revenue Minister in the Ministry of Gyan Singh Rarewala. From May 23, 1951 to March 18, 1952 he was Minister for Agriculture and PWD in the Ministry of Col. Raghubir Singh. In the first general election of 1952, he lost election in a 13-cornered contest. He was elected unanimously President of the PEPSU Pradesh Congress Committee for 1955-56 but with the merger of PEPSU into the State of Punjab on November 1, 1956, he was made Senior Vice-President of the Punjab Congress Committee for 1956-58. In 1956, he was elected member of Rajya Sabha and completed his term of six years till 1962. In general election held in 1962, he was elected to the Punjab Vidhan Sabha from Faridkot constituency by an overwhelming majority. On March 12, Chief Minister Pratap Singh Kairon inducted him into the Council of Ministers as Minister of State for Jails and Animal Husbandry. However, in the wake of Chinese aggression he stepped down but he continued to work in the organizational matters of the Congress.

Pratap Singh Kairon resigned from the chief ministership of Punjab on June 15, 1964, when Justice S.R. Das Commission's report went against him. Zail Singh was elected President of Punjab Pradesh Congress Committee for 1966-1972. In 1972 General Election, he won the Punjab Vidhan Sabha State Assembly seat from Anandpur Sahib-Ropar constituency. On March 15, 1972, he was elected leader of the Congress Party in the Assembly and on March 17 he became the Chief Minister of Punjab. During his tenure, the production of food grains went up to nine million tons. The net value of farm produce increased to Rs.12,040m. The community development package programmes saw their implementation at a rapid speed, including education, health, sanitation, agriculture, dairy farming, animal husbandry, soil and water conservation, rural communications and welfare of weaker sections of the society. These and other measures brought prosperity to the rural folk on an unprecedented scale. Industries were set up in backward areas of the State. In a homage to the unique personality of Guru Gobind Singh the Punjab Government laid a highway named after him, stretching 640 kms, which connected ninety-one spots associated with him. The Government also arranged interest-free loans for the actual cycle-*rickshaw* pullers to enable them to purchase their own *rickshaws*. Only the actual *rickshaw*-pullers were issued the driving licenses and the drivers alone were given the ownership registration in municipal areas. It created a feeling of self-respect amongst the *rickshaw*-pullers and eliminated their exploitation by the middlemen. Janata

Government assumed power following the results of the 1977 General Election. Punjab Government was dismissed along with some other Legislative Assemblies of Congress-run States. In this situation, Giani Zail Singh relinquished the chief ministership on May 1, 1977 and became loyal to Indira Gandhi during her dark days.

In January 1980, Giani Zail Singh won the election from the Hoshiarpur parliamentary constituency and entered the Seventh Lok Sabha. He was sworn in on January 14, 1980 as Minister for Home Affairs in Indira Gandhi's Cabinet. As Home Minister, he was quite firm in handling the complex problem of Assam and openly condemned the protagonists of "Khalistan" —a separate Sikh State. As Union Minister, he not only fostered communal harmony, national integration, maintained law and order but was also instrumental in increasing the pension and other facilities given to the freedom fighters and their families. He always tried to carry the Opposition with him. He said, "dissent is never a crime", but the Opposition must also appreciate the good actions of the government. To him, "politics and politicians without principles is poison".

On June 21, 1982, the Congress (I) Central Parliamentary Board nominated him as the Congress (I) candidate for the Presidentship of India. Thereupon, he resigned as the Home Minister of India on June 22 before he filed his nomination. He was elected to the highest office on July 15, 1982 securing 72.7 per cent votes, defeating his only rival Justice H.R. Khanna, the joint nominee of nine opposition parties, by 4,71,428 votes. He was administered the oath as the seventh Head of the State on July 25, 1982. He developed cordial relations with Prime Minister Indira Gandhi. On substantial issues, she consulted the President in Rashtrapati Bhavan. She always called on him before proceeding on a foreign tour and submitted her report on her return. But, somehow, she hesitated to discuss the Punjab situation with the President. However, the President, as he stated in his *Memoirs*, was "totally dissatisfied with the handling of the Punjab problem by the State Government and Prime Minister Indira Gandhi did not show much inclination to advise them to mend their ways. "I did not press the issue, but did not point out to her that all was not well with the functioning of the Government of Punjab. The picture was quite unsavoury", he wrote in his *Memoirs*. Amarinder Singh, a scion of the erstwhile ruling family of the Patiala State, made efforts to bring about an understanding between the Government and the agitating Akali Party, wrote the President in his *Memoirs*, but his efforts could not bear any fruit.

In December 1983, Prime Minister Indira Gandhi consulted President Zail Singh before he left on a tour to Czechoslovakia, Qatar and Bahrain. The President suggested the name of Swaran Singh to assist in this ticklish issue. The President told the Prime Minister that "the Punjab affairs were being mishandled for quite some time resulting in an impasse and it was unfortunate that she had not shown much understanding of this diagnosis". On his return from his tour of the three countries, the President met Swaran Singh who informed the President that an "understanding had been reached between the Government and the Akalis. It was agreed upon by the two sides that the Anandpur Sahib Resolution would be referred to a Parliamentary Committee, the contentious city of Chandigarh would be transferred to Punjab and the question of compensation to the Haryana State would be referred to judicial body. Under the agreement, Sikhs would be allowed to wear small *Kirpan*— their religious symbol—even during their airoplane flights. The President was told by Swaran Singh that the Central Government had accepted these propositions and an announcement would be made in this regard. But somehow a different situation arose.

The situation in Punjab went out of control. The agitation launched by the Akalis lasted for nineteen months, during which they had sent about 4,200 volunteers to court arrest. There were some differences between the President and the Prime Minister on the approach to be followed. The situation in Punjab went on deteriorating with the result that the Union

Government had to face the criticism for the 'rot'. The Government sent two ordinances to the President for his signatures without consulting him on the issues. The President felt that "it was a blunder on the part of the Government. One of the ordinances aimed at conferring powers on the Governor to declare any part of the State a disturbed area" and to authorize the Governor to call in the army for help in restoring law and order, without any reference to the Central Government. The President wanted to give a chance to the agitators to realize that since popular government had been shown the door, they should think of some common solution acceptable to them and the Government.

President Zail Singh advised some leaders to postpone the agitation when they met him. But unfortunately the impasse continued. The attitude of the Akalis hardened and they called for greater sacrifices from their followers proclaiming that the struggle would be a long-drawn affair. The Akalis supremo, Sant Harchand Singh Longowal, convened a meeting of Sikh intellectuals to discuss the 'crisis' facing the community. It was followed by a meeting of the Sikh ex-officers and men of the armed forces. The Akalis wanted the President to resign but President Zail Singh expressed his disinclination to heed to their advice, saying that "I was not elected by the Akalis alone, but by a vast electoral college consisting of Members of Parliament and all State Assemblies. People professing all religions belonging to all castes and coming from all parts of the country had voted me into office."

The Akalis threatened to embarrass the Government by holding demonstrations at the inaugural ceremony of the Ninth Asian Games. The Government made arrangements to stop them from coming to Delhi. This caused inconvenience and harassment even to those Sikhs who had absolutely no sympathy or link with the agitators. Those who felt the pinch of the "highhandedness of the Haryana police" started lending their sympathy to the hard-boiled elements. "The agitators and militants adopted the strategy of publicity offensive among the class of people and had been substantially successful in inciting their communal passions, feeding them exaggerated accounts of atrocities and discrimination against the Sikhs. But the Government had not taken sufficient notice of this propaganda. The Akalis were stirring communal sentiments of the Sikhs settled in foreign countries, because they were well-to-do and could be liberal with their money in the name of religion", later wrote Giani Zail Singh in his *Memoirs.*

In May 1984, when Prime Minister Indira Gandhi was given an idea of sending the police into the Golden Temple complex to flush out the militants entrenched therein, President Zail Singh told her that this course would not be proper and it will have serious repercussions. He suggested her subtle methods to dislodge the armed men from religious places. However, the Prime Minister did not spell the strategy she had in mind to meet the aggravating situation. On June 5, 1984, the Government launched an Operation Blue Star in the complex of the Golden Temple, Amritsar, for which the President didn't have the inkling even beforehand. There were again differences between the President and the Prime Minister on the possible approach which the Government could have followed to overcome the deterioration in the circumstances. The President particularly felt disturbed that the military action was taken on a day when the Temple complex was full of pilgrims assembled to observe the Martyrdom anniversary of Guru Arjun Dev. But the Government was more concerned about the exigencies of the circumstances.

In the wake of the Operation Blue Star, a good deal of pressure started mounting on the President to tender his resignation. President Zail Singh told the people that it was most unwise to turn the holy places into fortresses. *Gurudwaras,* he said, were meant for worship and spiritual solace and not for building arsenals. "Had the Sikh community, as a whole, raised its voice against the moves of a few short-sighted and misguided persons, all this humiliation and suffering could well have been avoided", wrote Giani Zail Singh later in his

Memoirs. "Of course, the Government too could not be exonerated of the damage caused by its policy of drift, indifferences to reality and the ultimate debacle, but I did not think my resignation would resolve the lost glory of the Sikhs", added President Giani Zail Singh in his *Memoirs*. His resignation, he said, as the Supreme Commander of the Armed Forces, might have generated a sense of guilt among the Serving Sikh members of the forces, giving rise to a feeling of persecution and a desire to square up things with the authority. President's resignation on this issue would have put the defence of the country in grave peril. It could have triggered a revolt in the armed forces providing an easy opportunity for a lightning attack from across the border. As President, he thought it his duty to defend and not endanger the integrity of the situation. Exigencies of the circumstances demanded President Zail Singh not to be sentimental and take a decision which could have tarnished the country's image.

President Zail Singh visited the Golden Temple twice and advised the Government to undertake various steps. In his broadcast to the nation, he expressed anguish over the chain of events which had led to the storming of the Golden Temple complex by the armed forces. Had the militants not turned the holy place into an embattled fortress, he said, so many arms and ammunition, the community and the country could have been saved from this agony. Now that the damage has been done, he pleaded that the services offered by the Government for repairs should be accepted without rancour. To use the religion for political purposes was grossly incorrect, he said, and to mix up politics with religion was quite inappropriate. Citing the saying of the Tenth Sikh Guru he said:

Some are accepted as Sanyasis, some are Shaven,
Others are Yogis or Brahmacharis, and Jatia,
Some are Hindus and others Muslims, and the latter
Are Rafzis, Immams and Shafis,
Know that all human beings are one.
Karta (the creator) and Karum (the beneficent) are the same;
Razak (the Provider) and Rahim (the Merciful) are the same,
Let no man, even by mistake, suppose there is a difference.

The President appealed to the Sikh community that they should draw inspiration from the works of the Guru as the Tenth Guru had said that "the Guru of the Sikhs after me will be *Guru Granth Sahib* and that there was a need for us to exercise caution so that we do not go astray".

Prime Minister Indira Gandhi met President Zail Singh at the airport when the latter left for Mauritius and People's Republic of Yemen. She wanted to discuss some important issues but could not go to Rashtrapati Bhavan owing to indisposition. From Mauritius the President proceeded to the People's Democratic Republic of Yemen and then to the Yemen Arab Republic. There, on October 31, 1984, his Private Secretary received a telephone call from New Delhi about the shoot-out at the residence of the Prime Minister and her having been wounded. It caused a great shock to the President and he immediately returned back to New Delhi. While in the airoplane journey he had a news from the BBC that Mrs Indira Gandhi had breathed her last. He got hold of a copy of the Constitution and consulted it afresh. He discussed the matter with his senior officers about the appointment of a new Prime Minister. His first thought was riveted on Rajiv Gandhi as, he thought, Rajiv would be acceptable to the majority party in the Lok Sabha. Well-being of the nation was his greatest concern. From New Delhi airport he straightaway left for All India Institute of Medical Sciences. On his way, he noticed some persons trying to commit arson and people with menacing faces were carrying burning torches at the end of their long bamboo poles. In All India Institute of Medical Sciences he expressed his deep sorrow and his condolences to Rajiv Gandhi. Rajiv was asked to come to Rashtrapati Bhavan where he was immediately sworn in as Prime Minister. He suggested Rajiv Gandhi to call in the Army to control lawlessness and vandalism which erupted following Indira Gandhi's assassination. A number of Sikhs became victims of this unprecedented wave of vengeance irrespective of their political creed or affiliation.

President Zail Singh has stated in his *Memoirs:* "After few days Prime Minister Rajiv Gandhi started avoiding me. Instead of meeting the President personally, Rajiv Gandhi started sending Arjun Singh". This became a topic of discussion both in the media and the Parliament. It was a deviation from the established convention for the Prime Minister to call on the President almost every week and keep the President informed of the important decisions of the Government." The President was kept in dark about the important foreign policy matters. However, Prime Minister Rajiv Gandhi called on President Zail Singh at Rashtrapati Bhavan on March 28, 1987 after a lapse of over two years. The President asked the Prime Minister about the reports of the Intelligence Bureau which he suddenly stopped getting. The Prime Minister's attention was also drawn to the reports from Indian ambassadors abroad which had stopped coming to him and to all this the President "attributed lack of trust in the Head of State". As a matter of fact, the discussion seemed quite acrimonious. President Zail Singh later gave a brief account of this in Chapter 40 of his *Memoirs*.

The President asked for detailed "factual information" on a number of aspects of Fairfax and Bofors. Prime Minister Rajiv Gandhi met the President on April 8, 1987 when they discussed the President-Prime Minister relationship. Prime Minister Rajiv Gandhi sent a note to the President and quoted from a note recorded by the first Prime Minister, Pandit Jawaharlal Nehru, written after consulting the Attorney-General, that "the President must act with the aid and advice of the Council of his Ministers and he could not act independently of that advice. The position of the President was weaker as compared to that of the British monarch. The President under our Constitution had no personal or other prerogatives, which the British King had. The fact that the President, unlike the King, was elected to his office for a term made no difference to his position. Prime Minister Rajiv Gandhi painstakingly quoted from Vols.7 and 8 of the Constituent Assembly Debates that every power conferred on the President had to be exercised according to the advice of the Ministers. He also referred to the Supreme Court judgment in *Shamsher Singh* vs *State of Punjab*, quoting Justice Krishna Iyer on the authority of Dr Ambedkar's view to the effect that a President who refused to accept ministerial advice would be committing violation of the Constitution. As a corollary to the open indifference shown by the Prime Minister to the President, a rumour was floated by some people that the President had a plan to replace Prime Minister Rajiv Gandhi with more reasonable and rational person. It seems that in view of all these circumstances, President Zail Singh did not feel it convenient to ask for a second term in office and his intention was made clear to the Prime Minister.

President Zail Singh received letters from certain prominent politicians providing the information gathered by them on Bofors Gun deal and Submarine deal. They wanted the President to ask the Prime Minister to step down from the office. Such letters were immediately forwarded to the Prime Minister. The President also sought opinion from some legal luminaries who were of the view that "it was a borderline case" when the "Prime Minister could get the benefit of doubt in a court of law. In such a case, acquittal was not difficult". Hence, it seems, the President didn't think it proper to give permission to prosecute the Prime Minister.

On December 22, 1986, a Bill to amend the Indian Postal Act of 1898, passed by both Houses of Parliament, was sent to the President for his assent. The Bill empowered the Government to intercept or detain or dispose of any article in the course of transmission if it is satisfied that it is necessary or expedient so to do in the interest of public safety or tranquility, the sovereignty or integrity of India, the security of the State, friendly relations with foreign States or public order or for preventing incitement to the commission of any offence, or on the concurrence of any public emergency. President Zail Singh found that the amended Bill was too sweeping in nature and wondered why the Government was keen in assuming the power to intercept any postal communication indiscriminately. He thought that the Bill undermined the fundamental freedom granted under the Constitution and was not in conformity with the Law Commission's 38th Report. It also went against the thrust of some Supreme Court judgments, and could mean that books, journals and periodicals could be subjectively censored and money orders could be withheld. He asked the Law Ministry to be more specific. The reply received did not satisfy the President. He once again wrote to the Government urging them to take a view consistent with the right to freedom of speech and expression guaranteed under the Constitution and the principles of natural justice. He didn't give his assent to the Bill, as, in his opinion, it militated against the basic freedom guaranteed to the citizens.

His term came to an end on July 25, 1987. After retirement he settled down in Delhi. He met with a serious accident and breathed his last on December 25, 1994. To conclude, Giani Zail Singh had a very humble beginning. Brought up in a religious ambience he was fired with patriotic fervour and because of his penchant for opposition of injustice, he had to undergo a long prison term under inhuman conditions. As the President of India, he braced through some problems but he exercised his Constitutional authority with great patience and equanimity. He cautioned the people, especially the Sikh militants, and reminded them of the saying in Guru *Granth Sahib*:

List all, the truth I hereby proclaim;
Only those practicing loving devotion shall attain God.

14

Ramaswami Venkataraman

1910-2009

Tenure as President
25 July 1987-25 July 1992
Votes Secured: 740,148
Nearest Rival
Justice V.R. Krishna Iyer
Votes Secured: 281,558

Dr Ramaswami Venkataraman, who succeeded Giani Zail Singh, as the eighth President of India, had been a leading lawyer who specialized in Industrial Relations Law. He is remembered as the Father of Industrialization of Tamil Nadu. With his deep knowledge of law and the Constitution of India he steered clear through the political as well as sensitive years and took momentous decisions involving significant challenging constitutional and political issues, which included the dispatch of Indian troops to Sri Lanka, the Bofors Gun deal, the Stock Scam and the Defamation Bill.

Born on December 4, 1910, in Rajamadam village, Thanjavur District in Tamil Nadu, Ramaswami Venkataraman had a distinguished academic career. Educated locally and in the city of the then Madras, Venkataram obtained his Master degree in Economics from Madras University. He later qualified in Law from the Law College, Madras (now, Chennai). He enrolled himself as an advocate of the Madras High Court in 1935 and later of the Supreme Court of India in 1951. While practicing law, Venkataraman was drawn into the movement for India's freedom from Britain's colonial subjugation. Because of his active participation in the Quit India Movement he was arrested and incarcerated for two years in Vellore Central Jail. In 1935, he was elected a member of the United Nations Administrative Tribunal by the United Nations General Assembly. He was a member of the Tribunal from 1955 to 1979 and its President from 1968 to 1979. During this period, he rendered several important judgments. He was one of penal of lawyers deputed by the Government of India in 1946 to defend Indian nationals in Malaya and Singapore charged with the offences of collaboration with the Japanese during World War II. From 1947 to 1950 he served as Secretary of the Madras Province Bar Federation.

During his legal career, Venkataraman acquired an abiding interest in the law pertaining to labour. On his release from prison in 1944, he took up the organization of the Labour Section of the Tamil Nadu Congress Committee. In 1949, he initiated the publication of the *Labour Law Journal* which includes important decisions pertaining to labour. He was intimately associated with trade union activity. He founded and led several unions of plantation workers, estate staff, dock workers, railway workers and working journalists. He also took keen interest in the condition of agricultural workers in his home district of Thanjavur. He was leader of the Indian Delegation to the 42nd Session of the International Labour Conference in Vienna in 1978.

Venkataraman's early legal training had stood him in good stead in his career. The habit of studying the files carefully instead of glancing at them superficiously was a habit which he had developed over the years. The experience, gained by practice at the Bar, helped him later. As President, on September 2, 1989, at the inaugural ceremony of Madras Advocates Association, he cautioned against liberal exercise of the writ jurisdiction when alternative remedies were available so that the highest courts may not be choked with work. He appealed to the Bar to cooperate in reducing the length of hearing of cases and help quicker administration of justice.

In fact, Venkataraman started his career at the grass-root level and then became a trade union lawyer. His active participation in parliamentary proceedings attracted the attention of Prime Minister Jawaharlal Nehru. From nearly a decade, Nehru assigned Venkataraman the privilege of representing India as delegate to the United Nations General Assembly. He was later appointed Industry Minister under K. Kamaraj, and successively to the offices of Member of the Union Planning Commission, Union Finance Minister, and Union Defence Minister.

In August 1984, Venkataraman was elected Vice-President of India. He was simultaneously Chairman of the Rajya Sabha. As Chairman, he was cordial and firm with everyone across the benches, pulling members up for inadvertencies as much as for intentional misconduct during Question Hour; the 'hour' that he scrupulously spent in the House. Prolixity, additional supplementaries, 'irregular' Calling Attention Notices, Adjournment Motions would be summarily put down. Nothing will go on record, nothing was heard in the familiar high-pitched voice on the Chair whenever someone broke the decorum of the proceedings by speaking without authority. Members doing a 'walkout' would invariably hear the Chairman saying with a smile "Walkng out". All right, anyway, attendance is optional ... making the MP look and feel utterly un-heroic. Predictably, Venkataram earned the left-handed title of "Headmaster".

As Vice-President, he was also Chairman of the Jury for the Jawaharlal Nehru Award for International Understanding and of the International Jury for the Indira Gandhi Prize for Peace, Disarmament and Development. He was Vice-Chairman of the Jawaharlal Nehru Memorial Fund; Trustee, Indira Gandhi Memorial Trust; President, Indian Institute of Public Administration; Chancellor, Gandhigram Rural Institute; Chancellor, University of Delhi; Chancellor, Punjab University and President of the Indian Council for Cultural Relations.

In 1986, he succeeded Giani Zail Singh as the President of India as nominee of the Congress Party getting 4,690 votes of electoral college of the value of 740,148 votes against 1,439 votes of the value of 281,550 by Justice V.R. Krishna Iyer.

During his meetings with the Prime Minister, the President used to discuss not only matters concerning national and international affairs but also many other things concerning life in general. He gave him his own observations about the public life and situation in the country in general. Wherever the situation demanded, the matters to which the President's attention was drawn by the politicians, academicians and others, were also referred to. Once, while on his private visit to Shimla, he wrote to Prime Minister Rajiv Gandhi to draw his attention to the spiraling inflation and suggested that the Government may undertake measures to correct the situation. On one occasion, Rajiv Gandhi was totally obsessed by the day-to-day problems and was in a depressed mood. The President advised him to take a detached view and should not get involved emotionally in every issue. He sent him a copy of *Bhaja Govindam* along with Rajagopalachari's English commentary.

It was during President Venkataraman's tenure that two ticklish issues were referred to him by Prime Minister Rajiv Gandhi. One was regarding enhanced pension to past presidents from July 1987 and another Punjab. The enhanced pension to president was expected to operate prospectively from the date of the order or retrospectively from the date when living president demitted office. About the situation in Punjab, the President cautioned the Prime Minister against introduction of emergency provisions in Punjab. He suggested amending Article 356 of the Constitution, assuming powers to extend President's Rule beyond one year up to a maximum of three years and as a more appropriate course. After the Rajiv-Longowal Agreement, elections were held in Punjab and an Akali Government was formed under Surjeet Singh Barnala. The violence and terrorism that plagued Punjab did not abate but escalated and there was a complete breakdown of law and order situation. Hence, President's Rule was imposed on Punjab in May 1987 but the legislature was kept in suspended animation in the hope that a popular government could be revived if the situation improved.

There was an alarming deterioration in the law and order situation in Punjab. The Government contemplated the re-introduction of internal disturbance as a ground for declaring emergency and to bring in the Constitution Amendment Bill in respect of the whole of Punjab or such parts of Punjab as may be specified. Notwithstanding the strenuous efforts by the Opposition, the 59th Constitution Amendment Bill was adopted by both Houses of Parliament and was referred to the President. Editorials in newspapers counseled the President to withhold extension or return the Bill for reconsideration or refer the issue to the Supreme Court under Article 143 of the Constitution. Leaders of the Opposition presented a memorandum to the President alleging undue haste, erosion of democratic and constitutional rights, discrimination against Punjab and denial of fundamental rights to its people, and possible abuse by bureaucracy. The President was under pressure from all sides. He was in a dilemma as to what course he should follow on that occasion to "preserve, protect and defend the Constitution." He pondered over and thought about the issues day and night. He again referred to Article 111 of the Constitution even though he was quite familiar with its provisions. He came across sub-section (2) of Article 368 which left the President with no option but to give assent to an amendment to the Constitution adopted in accordance with the Article. He also felt convinced that it was beyond the scope of the authority of the President to go into the legal validity of a Bill which was duly adopted by the Parliament and that if there was any infirmity it was within the jurisprudence of the courts to pronounce it. He, therefore, discussed the issue with the Attorney-General who also agreed with the President. In view of all this, the President gave an assent to the Bill.

When leaders of the Opposition parties in Parliament presented him a memorandum demanding a fresh probe into the Bofors gun deal in the light of certain startling disclosures appearing in the well-known and sober daily, *The Hindu*, and urged him an immediate action, the President politely accepted the memorandum and said that he would study its contents. He, however, reminded them the limitation of his office and passed on the memorandum to the Prime Minister.

There were occasions when President Venkataraman acted in his own way leaving aside the protocol. To him, protocol is observed in official formalities and etiquette. Once he received Rajiv Gandhi at the Airport on the latter's return from Sri Lanka after dastardly attack on him by one man during the Guard of Honour. On May 2, 1988, he also stepped down from the dais and walked up to the ailing Raj Kapoor to present him the Dada Saheb Phalke Award. These were instances of courtesy overriding convention. Such acts were appreciated by the press and the public.

While participating in a function at the Sankara Higher Secondary School in Chennai, President Venkataraman condemned the practice of charging capitation fee for admission to schools and colleges. He said, "If I had the authority of a director I would have abolished all schools which collected capitation fees ... It is far better to have a fewer schools with better standards than institutions thriving on immoral behaviour." He lamented that most of the schools have become business houses as people invested a little money and set up educational institutions only to make huge profit by extorting money from the parents.

As President, he used to receive a number of letters from the public. He made it a system that every letter addressed to him was sent by his staff to him. Ordinary letters were opened by the staff, while letters marked personal or 'confidential' were put up unopened. But the President insisted that the *dak* should reach him. Once he received a heart-rending letter in Urdu from a resident of Amritsar giving a graphic account of "Bloodbath in Punjab". This letter was referred to the then Prime Minister to apprise him of the situation and the ground realities in Punjab.

As President, he visited the erstwhile Soviet Russia, Bhutan, Zimbabwe, Zambia, Tanzania, Japan, Seychelles, Vietnam, U.K, The Netherlands, Finland, Cyprus and Czechoslovakia. His visit to Soviet Russia, where he described the Festival of India as "a voyage to discovery" of understanding and friendship, was hailed as yet another milestone in the ever-growing friendship between India and the Soviet Union. His visit to other countries paved the way for cementing the bond of friendship with India. He portrayed many-splendoured image of India to all such countries. Quoting *Rig Veda*, in his address to the Soviet audience, he said

Meet together, talk together,
May your minds comprehend alike,
Common be your action and achievement,
Common be your thoughts and intentions,
Common be the wishes of your hearts.

In his addresses on the eve of the Republic Day and Independence Day, he emphasized the responsibilities of political parties for ensuring free and fair elections. He appealed to all political parties and groups as well as administrators and police in-charge of elections to regard themselves as trustees of the voters' sovereignty and to act with integrity and impartiality.

The mercy petition of Kehar Singh in the Indira Gandhi assassination case came to him under Article 72 of the Constitution. The Cabinet Minister conveyed to him the advice of the Government to reject the petition. The Government felt that there should be no interference with the decision of the Supreme Court rejecting the appeal of the condemned prisoner. The President consulted the Attorney-General on the legality and propriety of rejecting the mercy petition. In the meantime, the Supreme Court dismissed the special leave petition moved on behalf of Kehar Singh. The President got a copy of the order from the Attorney-General and thereafter accepted the recommendation of the Home Minister to reject the mercy petition, but said that it would be better if the sentence was not carried out before Guru Nanak's Birthday on November 23.

The President was particular about the legality of any issue which came to him. Rajendra Kumar Jindal, a resident of Delhi, filed an application before the President seeking the disqualification of 100 MPs on the ground that they were sitting members of the Seventh Lok Sabha and were holding "offices of profit" and therefore were not competent to contest the election to the Eighth Lok Sabha. The President referred the matter under Article 103 (1) of the Constitution. The Election Commission also referred to the decision of the Supreme Court that membership of Parliament was not an office of profit. Therefore, Jindal's petition was rejected by the President on March 23, 1989.

On May 11, 1989, Rashtrapati Bhavan received a letter from a senior advocate of the Supreme Court, requesting sanction under the Prevention of Corruption Act for the prosecution of Prime Minister Rajiv Gandhi for corruption and bribery. It alleged that the Prime Minister was guilty of corruption in the Bofor's gun deal. The Attorney-General was consulted. It was found that though the Constitution provides that the Prime Minister shall be appointed by the President and the Ministers shall hold office during the pleasure of the President, the Council of Ministers cannot be removed as long as it enjoys the confidence of the House of the People. Though based on the judgment of the Supreme Court in *Karunanidhi*'s case, the President was the sanctioning authority for the prosecution of the Prime Minister and based on *Antulay*'s case the President should act on his discretion and not on the advice of the Council of Ministers. The petition was rejected as it was based on the reports of newspapers and there was no evidence connecting the Prime Minister with the receipt or acceptance of bribe and that the allegations were just arguments based on surmise.

In the opinion of President Venkataraman, "Governor plays an important role in the affairs of their respective states. The ship of the States has to cross stormy rapids and it is the responsibility of the helmsman and head of the government to navigate those rapids", he said, adding that "the duty of the governors, as head of the States, is to provide the steady support of ballast". In an annual Conference of Governors in 1989, he told the Governors that their earlier role as ceremonial Heads of State had changed and that they were called upon to shoulder the responsibility of direct administration in states under President's Rule and that they should, therefore, exercise judgments with extreme care.

On November 28, 1989, it became clear that the Congress had lost even though the entire results had not come out. Soli J Sorabjee, former Solicitor-General and an expert in Constitutional law, wrote in an article that the British precedence had established that when a ruling party had been defeated in any general election, only the Opposition should be called to form the Government. President Venkataraman saw substance in the plea that a defeated ruling party should not be asked to form the Ministry as it had forfeited the mandate of the people. Ultimately, it turned out that the Congress was the largest single party with 194 members but there was an apprehension of "Hung Parliament" as no party had the absolute majority. Therefore, President Venkataraman advised the Cabinet to immediately tender its resignation. Thus, V.P. Singh, leader of Janata Dal, the second largest party/group, was invited to form the Government.

When Prime Minister Narasimha Rao issued an appeal for austerity in the administration in view of the continuing fiscal crisis, President Venkataraman effected a cut of 10 per cent in his own salary. Two imported cars in Rashtrapati Bhavan were reserved for use of the President and visiting dignitaries and the remaining cars were auctioned.

President Venkataraman retired in July 1992 after completing his tenure. In his farewell address in the Central Hall of Parliament he compared the powers of the President to an emergency lamp, which came into operation when power failed and became dormant when power was restored. He said that the responsibility of the administration of the country rested with the Prime Minister who carried the confidence of the Parliament and the President was not an appellate or a supervisory authority over the Prime Minister and the Cabinet.

In view of his distinguished contributions to law, the universities of Madras, Nagarjuna and Burdwan conferred on him the Doctorate of Law (*Honoris Causa*). He had been the Honorary Fellow of the Madras Medical College, Doctor of Social Science from the University of Roorkee. He had been the recipient of Soviet Land Prize for his travelogue on Shri Kamaraj's visit to the Socialist countries and Souvenir from the Secretary-General of the United Nations for distinguished service as President of the U.N. Administrative Tribunal. The title of *Sat Seva Ratnam* had also been conferred on him by His Holiness Sankaracharya of Kancheepuram.

At the age of 96, following multiple organ failure after two weeks of hospitalisation, the former President Venkataram left for a heavenly abode on January 27, 2009. The Union Cabinet decided to accord a state funeral to Venkataraman near Ekta Sthal at 4.3 pm.

Ramaswamy Venkataraman's role as President was like a Headmaster, as he himself said to counsel the children, in his acceptance speech after he was sworn in as the President—what to do and what not to do. His was an eventful tenure that saw three prime ministers—V.P. Singh, Chandra Shekhar and P.V. Narasimha Rao—being sworn in, when two years of coalition politics made its beginning in India. Though a stickler for rules and procedures, he wanted changes in the Constitution despite the fact that he himself had been the member of the Constituent Assembly that drafted it. His experience with coalition politics led to his openly advocating a national government for political stability in case of a fractured verdict. President Venkataraman even spoke against the coalition form of government.

15

Shankar Dayal Sharma

Tenure as President
25 July 1992-25 July 1997
Votes Secured: 675,864
Nearest Rival
G.G. Swell
Votes Secured: 346,485

1918-1999

Dr Shankar Dayal Sharma, the ninth President of India, had been a great Sanskrit scholar, an educationist, a distinguished intellectual, a widely respected national leader, an avid reader of Vedas, a symbol of patience, ascetic simplicity and kindness, and a combination of patriotism and catholicity.

Shankar Dayal was born on August 19, 1918 in the Misran Mohalla of Bhopal in Madhya Pradesh. His father, Pandit Khushi Ram Sharma, was an Ayurvedic practitioner of repute and was known for his skill in curing diseases and showed remarkable tenacity and penetrating insight in diagnosing the chronic diseases. His mother was a devout Brahmin lady. As a boy, Shankar Dayal was sober. His father used to take him on picnic parties to neighbouring hill areas in Bhopal which was then picturesque in many of nature's bounties. The surrounding hillocks the famous Bhopal lake, rows of trees, shrubs and bushes gave an idyllic air to the environment. As the young Shankar Dayal accompanied his father to the picnic parties he breathed the air with a philosophical stance and it filled the boy's mind with sublime thoughts.

At an early age, Shankar Dayal came in contact with Pandit Jamna Prasad, a man of erudition, who was well-versed in

Persian and who initiated the young boy to the flavour and richness of Persian and Urdu. Bhopal, at that time, was a princely State in India. The atmosphere—political environmental and ethnic—was charged with mediocrity, political backwardness and narrow sectarian consideration. Outside the State, in India, Mahatma Gandhi's Khilafat and Non-Cooperation movements did find the reverberation in Bhopal. Besides, the "cow slaughter", and "music before mosques" and the "*Shuddhi*" movement also found their echoes in the State. When the boy entered the primary school, called Krishna Pathshala, Brijisia, he had to undergo learning by rote—the conventional method of the primary school teaching. Some important changes in the political and social conditions began to take place. Thus, his mind was steeped in classical culture that came to him through his home. He heard the faint echoes of the defunct Khilafat Movement. Mahatma Gandhi's visit to Bhopal in 1928 saw the opening to Khadi Bhandar.

At the age of 15, Shanker Dayal passed his matriculation examination and joined St. John College at Agra. There he took part in curricular activities with a great gusto. In Agra, he played tennis for the first time and his aim was to excel. He loved poetry in Hindi, Urdu and English. Once he was invited to address a weekly meeting of representative students. He hesitated, then stood up to speak, uttered a word, repeated it thrice, and could not proceed with a sentence. His legs trembled and the beads of perspiration showed on his face. Nervous beyond words, Shankar Dayal, destined to become India's President, who would address public meetings of millions of people, stood flabbergasted. He then sat down never to be let down. He made up his mind to excel in this art. So, he practiced the art of oratory in which he spoke from the heart.

Shankar Dayal passed the intermediate examination in second division. He felt frustrated and left Agra. He made up his mind to seek nothing but the best in academic achievement. Religion attracted him but the intellectual quests, which tradition of Western learning opened out before him, were irresistible. He joined the Kayastha Pathshala affiliated to Allahabad University for B.A. course. In Allahabad, at that time, a significant stir had begun in university students circle. Jawaharlal Nehru used to address study circle meetings of university students some times in Swaraj Bhawan and elsewhere. Young Shankar Dayal was drawn in the magnetic touch in Nehru's personality and was readily responsive to the leader's speeches on socialism and nationalism, set within the context of international situation. He had the opportunity of observing Jawaharlal Nehru at close quarters. The nation was behind Mahatma Gandhi, and Nehru was behind Gandhi. He listened to the speeches of Jawaharlal quite carefully. He passed his B.A examination in 1937 from Allahabad University.

With Nehru's influence, young Shankar Dayal got more and more drawn into the vortex of international events mentally. Having passed his B.A. from Allahabad Shanker Dayal moved forward into new pastures. He left Allahabad to join Lucknow University where he joined M.A course in English literature. Literature meant not merely a medium of enjoyment of the magic of words but an accepted instrument of awakening the human mind to higher destiny. English literature, with its Shakespeare, Milton, Wordsworth, Dickens, Eliot, etc. prepared the emotional subsoil in Shankar Dayal's personality for a splendid blending of finer sensibilities of culture and harsh realities of politics. In 1939, he passed his M.A examination with distinction. The study of literature whetted his appetite for a taste of Sanskrit and Hindi literature. He took the M.A examination in both the subjects and passed with credit.

Simultaneously, Shanker Dayal felt drawn to legal studies. He joined LL.M, fathomed the depth of legal quibbling to fish out the law of natural justice and was declared as a top -notcher first class in the examination at the age of 23. He was awarded Chakravarti Gold Medal and was appointed lecturer in the University to teach Constitutional Law and the Law of Torts. So deep was his legal knowledge that the Head of Law, Dr Ramanugraha Singh, used to say that "Shanker Dayal would one day make a mark in the field of international law". It so happened that one day as Dr Singh was lecturing on Muslim Law, a student raised queries which he was unable to answer. He said he was unable to locate the context but suggested to his students to contact Shanker Dayal who was an authority on law. Through his amiable behaviour not only did he win his Vice-Chancellor's favour but also the regard and affection of his fellow professors despite the rivalries which are natural among university dons.

These were the days of the 1942 Quit India Movement. Lucknow University did register the impact on an appreciable scale. The faculty members in the university did their best to help the movement in different ways. Shanker Dayal was seized of the situation created by the Quit India Movement and contributed to its activities. He prepared the student community intellectually to keep abreast with the Quit India Movement. As Chief Editor of *Light & Learning* he wrote in its editorial once: "We must go to the toiling masses and make them conscious of their rights and their high destiny and human beings. We must try to make them fit citizens of India which shall be free one day and great again, leading an Asiatic federation of great nations by taking light to them." Thus, the students around him got the mental ignition of freedom and independence for India. Simultaneously, Shanker Dayal was active in the sphere of sports as well. In swimming competitions, both as a post-graduate student as well as a teacher, he always won laurel. In wrestling bouts, too, he could not yield the ground; in long-jumps and in swift race he was agile and ebullient, and in stamina he had the vitality of a horse.

The pull towards academic achievements was great on Shanker Dayal's mind. In 1948, he enrolled himself in the Cambridge University as an advanced research student in the law faculty for Ph.D. Within 2-3 years, he completed his thesis for Ph.D. His supervisor and examiners were so impressed by his thesis that he was exempted from taking the Viva. He also obtained his Bar-at-Law from Lincoln's Inn. His academic achievement was recognized in the United States also. The Harvard Law School awarded him the Brandes

Fellowship (1947-48). He began contributing articles in international law journals and returned to India on October 16, 1948.

After winning laurels abroad, Shanker Dayal returned to India on October 16, 1948. With an array of degrees crowning his stay abroad, he was received with great enthusiasm by Lucknow University which, at once, appointed him as the Reader in Law. Although the appointment meant elevation in the university hierarchy, Dr Sharma's heart was elsewhere. His unconscious mind carried the flaming memories of Nehru's proximity— his musing speeches, his burning passion for the upliftment of the toiling masses. Later, his own style of public speeches shows the mark of Nehru's phrases. He made up his mind to shed the academic gown and to jump into the fray of the Bhopal state merger movement. In January 1949, he was arrested while attempting to make a speech. Almost 240 political prisoners were arrested in connection with the merger movement and lodged at Bairagarh in the barracks which were originally meant for the Italian and German prisoners of war.

Dr Sharma was President of Madhya Pradesh Congress Committee from 1967 to 1968, a spell which gave him an insight into the intricacies of the Congress organization at the State level. On January 17, 1968, S. Nijalingappa appointed Dr Sharma to the Working Committee of the Indian National Congress. Four months later, on April 3, 1968, he was appointed as one of the General Secretaries of the AICC. As AICC's Secretary he knew that the economic situation in India in the sixties was in a bad shape. The value of the rupee had plummeted with two wars fought in the recent past: with China in 1962, and Pakistan in 1965. When Nijalingappa and his colleagues were greatly incensed over the defeat of Sanjeeva Reddy as presidential candidate at the hands of Indira Gandhi's candidate V.V. Giri, Dr Sharma, as General Secretary, was discharging his duties unmindful of the shifting stands in the Congress politics. He was asked by Nijalingappa to submit his resignation from the general secretaryship which he promptly did. Indira Gandhi did not like this. The Congress was divided. Nijalingappa was removed as Congress President from the group led by Indira Gandhi. Indira Gandhi reconstituted her Working Committee which included Dr Sharma.

On May 11, 1972, Dr Sharma took over as President of the Congress Party led by Indira Gandhi. In the Lok Sabha mid-term election of 1971, Dr Sharma was elected as a Member of Parliament. In 1973, he was again elected President of the Indian National Congress for the second time. In his Presidential Address, Dr Sharma regretted the continuous trend of policy distortion and pointed out that in spite of hundreds of thousands of rupees being pumped into the countryside since Independence the benefits could not trickle down to the poorer section of the people. He warned that the price situation would assume a serious proportion unless the private sector was firmly dealt with, and a strict survey over bank credit to commercial sector duly maintained. In 1974, he was inducted in the Union Cabinet as Minister of Communication. From 1974 to 1977, Dr Sharma continued to be in the Central Cabinet as Minister of Communications. He was a Minister in Indira Gandhi's Cabinet during the Emergency period 1975-77. As a disciplined colleague of Indira Gandhi, he stood by her. During the 1977 Lok Sabha election, he faced electoral defeat along with Indira Gandhi. On August 27, 1984 he was appointed Governor of Andhra Pradesh when Governor Ram Lal announced his resignation.

The 1984 "Operation Bluestar", launched by the Central Government against the Sikh terrorists, led to wide-ranging repercussions. Prime Minister Indira Gandhi was assassinated and in August 1985 Dr Sharma's daughter Geetanjali and son-in-law Lalit Makan were shot dead by militants in their house. The grief froze into icebergs floating in the perennial spirit of his inner life. His deep study of the *Bhagavad Gita* cushioned his mind against this bolt from the skies. Both Dr Sharma and his wife, Vimla, faced the grim tragedy with stoic fortitude. He was appointed Governor of Maharashtra where he remained from 1986 to 1987.

In 1987, Dr Sharma took over as the Vice-President of India and Chairman of Rajya Sabha. The Opposition parties joined hands with the Congress Party in deciding to support Dr Sharma since he had been a jurist and a constitutionalist. His election, thus, was a smooth affair. He carried on his duties as Chairman of Rajya Sabha in an impartial manner. On February 23, 1988, the Congress Party members in the Rajya Sabha defied a ruling by the Chairman. But Dr Sharma still allowed P. U;pendra, Telugu Desam member to raise the issue of ostentatious and unwarranted, wasteful expenditure in Raj Bhawan by the Governor Kumudben Joshi. The Congress members pressed their protest on the plea that the Governor's wasteful expenditure could not be discussed in Rajya Sabha. The Chair held that a member had the freedom to express his views. So vociferous was the protest by the Congress Party members that in sheer exasperation Dr Sharma remarked to the Congress members if they wish, he could resign from the post of Chairman and Vice-President. He said: "I am here to defend the right of a member to express his views". Next day, the veteran leader, Kamlapati Tripathi, wrote a letter to Prime Minister Rajiv Gandhi asking him to apologise to Dr Sharma on behalf of the irate Congress members whose unbecoming conduct caused much distress to Dr Sharma. Later, leader of the House, N.D. Tiwari, expressed regret over what had happened earlier.

On July 16, 1962 Dr Sharma was declared elected President of India as nominee of Congress Party, supported by Leftist parties. He was sworn in for this highest post on July 25, 1992. He took the oath in Hindi and English as he felt that in India English is the only link language between different regions. At public functions he mostly spoke in English. As a constitutional expert and a jurist he received appreciation from Congress and non-Congress citizens who believed that the letter and spirit of the Indian Constitution was safe in his hands.

In 1993, at a ceremony at Shravanabelagola, the honour of Dharma Ratnaker was conferred on him. In July 1993, the University of Ukraine conferred on him the Doctorate of that

University (*honoris clausa*). Lal Bahadur Shastri Sanskrit Vidyapeeth, New Delhi (a deemed university) decided to confer on Dr Sharma its honorary degree of Vachaspati.

Dr Sharma completed his term as ninth President of India on July 24, 1997 to be succeeded by President K.R. Narayanan. In his farewell address to the nation he called upon the people to uphold the "moral and ethical values of our civilization—values illumined during our freedom struggle and personified by the Father of our Nation, Mahatma Gandhi. Himself a great freedom fighter, he knew that country's Independence was the culmination and the sustained efforts of people belonging to all religions and castes. Therefore, he impressed upon the nation the centrality of "secularism—the respect for all religions" in our national creed.

The country found Dr Sharma the perfect constitutional Head of State. Quietly, but very effectively, he made his presence felt wherever the political leaders failed to rise to the occasion. The events which cropped up during Dr Sharma's tenure were, at times, quite stormy but he played the role of a father-figure always reminding ethical and moral values to our leaders. When Babri Masjid was demolished he reminded P.V. Narasimha Rao the responsibility of the Government to protect every citizen. In times of scams and scandals, he kept reminding the leaders of their ethical obligations.

The Central Bureau of Investigation (CBI) found the Himachal Pradesh Governor, Shiela Kaul, involved in the out-of-turn housing allotment scandal which had been under the Supreme Court's continuing critical scrutiny. In spite of this, the Narasimha Rao Government took the stand that no action was needed till the Court considered the parameters of the immunity enjoyed by a Governor. President Dr Shanker Dayal Sharma retrieved the situation by taking the stand that in keeping with the first principles of Constitutional propriety, Kaul should quit "without further ado". He made it unequivocally clear that this immunity cannot be used at the expense of the dignity of the office of the Governor, and that was the sufficient reason for the Governor to step down. By making his views public, the President helped in strengthening the reformist trend.

In May 1996, India's strong electorate consisting of 591.5 million voted to elect the Eleventh Parliament, but the net result of the whole exercise was a hopeless "Hung House". In the absence of a clear mandate the Bharatiya Janata Party (BJP) emerged the single largest party in the 543-member House, bagging 177 seats. The ruling Indian National Congress (INC), which was a pale shadow of the party that ruled Independent India for over four decades, was thrown out of power and was marginalized with 135 seats. In this situation, President Sharma invited Atal Bihar Vajpayee of the BJP to form the Government on the ground that the BJP was the single largest party, after the United Front failed to produce a letter of support from the Congress.

Dr Shanker Dayal Sharma expired on December 26, 1999. He was scholar of ancient traditions inheriting spiritual writings of India. Although a Congressman throughout his life, as President he kept himself above partisan politics. His counsel was available to the Government whenever any constitutional issue arose or when a reference was made to him. He invariably exercised his moral authority protecting the Constitution of India from any infringement. His vision and political acumen gave the right direction to the nation. Equipped with varied fields like law, literature, he was able to brace through many upheavals with dignity and equanimity. He wrote more than fifteen books. His Convocation Addresses, published in a book, are marked by erudition and ethical tone. In them lurks the fond heart of a personality which hungered for knowledge more and more, and like his motto "excelsior", he continued to search for it in aspirations, intellectual and spiritual.

16

K. R. Narayanan

Tenure as President
25 July 1997-25 July 2002
Votes Secured: 956,290
Nearest Rival
T.N. Seshan
Votes Secured: 50,631

1920-2005

The election of K.R Narayanan as the nation's tenth President of India was reduced to a mere formality after three major political formations decided to sponsor his nomination. His victory by 94.97 per cent of the vote value with a tally of 956,290 votes as against 50,631 value of votes secured by his opponent, i.e. 5.03 per cent of the total, is fully reflective of his near-unanimous acceptability of the elected Members of Parliament and the State Legislatures, as well as his non-impeachable credentials for the highest Constitutional office in consonance with the majesty and dignity of the office—the necessary transcendence of party barriers demanded by the high office. Though the political parties supporting Narayanan projected his caste label, but it had been unfair to Narayanan and all that he achieved against heavy odds. The fact that a member of the *dalit* community occupied the highest position when the nation celebrated the golden jubilee of its Independence was indicative of the message to the younger generation that hard work and dedication and not the glamour of the caste takes one to this stage in the present-day India. A scholar, a teacher, a writer, and an outstanding diplomat, a talented minister, and, above all, a humble human being, his life had been a saga of struggle and dedication which put a question mark on the belief that the downtrodden cannot expect justice in India. His elevation to the highest post was a testimony to the fact that with merit one can rise to the pinnacle of glory regardless of one's caste or creed.

Kocheril Raman Narayanan was the fourth of the seven children of Raman Vaidyan, a *dalit* traditional medical practitioner. He was born on October 27, 1920 in Uhavoor village in Kottayam District of Kerala, which was predominantly a Christian locality, little different from other villages of central Kerala. Most of its inhabitants were small farmers who grew paddy, coconut, tapioca, banana and other such crops in their small plots. His family experienced extreme social and economic hardship. His father could never make enough money to support his large family, but his uneducated mother, sister Gouri, and brother Neelakantan were keen on ensuring the best possible education to Narayanan.

At the age of four, Narayanan was sent to the nearest primary school at a place called Kurichittanam. Penury placed extreme limitations on Narayanan's educational pursuits. He had to walk 10-15 kms every day to his schools in Uzhavoor, Koothalukulum and Kuruvilangadu, and later, for his intermediate course, to the C.M.S College in Kottayam. When he was unable to attend classes regularly, as his father could not afford to pay the fees before the 10th of every month, he was frequently punished. At times, he had to stand on the bench in front of the whole class. Since he was unable to buy books, he would read the books again and again whatever he could lay hand on and take notes. Despite all this, he had the best of education in the erstwhile princely State of Travancore. He studied on merit scholarships from the intermediate level (11th standard) and in 1943 passed the B.A (Literature) Honours examination from the Maharaja's College in Thiruvananthapuram, securing 60 per cent marks and the first rank. But he was denied the job of a lecturer in the same college as he didn't belong to the higher caste. Instead, the then Vice-Chancellor, Dewan of Travancore, C.P. Ramaswami Aiyar, offered him a clerical post in the University and a book with Rs.100. Narayanan did not go to the convocation to collect his degree. It was after 50 years, when he returned to the Senate as Vice-President that he accepted the degree and when the officials "begged" him to accept it.

After unsuccessful attempts to become a full-time lecturer, Narayanan worked for a while as a teacher on a leave vacancy. Then he left for Delhi to try and become a journalist. After working as an assistant in a government office, which earned him Rs.250 he quit and joined a Delhi-based economic weekly, *Commerce and Industry*, edited by Dr Lanka Sundaram, as a journalist on a salary of Rs.100. For some time, he worked as sub-editor in *The Hindu* and later as reporter in *The Times of India*, Bombay (now, Mumbai), where he had the rare distinction of once interviewing Mahatma Gandhi.

While working in *The Economic Weekly* he wrote a letter to J.R.D. Tata and sought scholarship which eventually took him to the London School of Economics and Political Science. There he was taught by the world famous political thinker, Prof Harold Laski. In 1948, he completed his three-year economics degree in two years with first class honours, specializing in political science. During that period, he also worked as the London Correspondent of the *Social Welfare Weekly*, Bombay, which was edited by K.M. Munshi. Though Prof. Laski was much impressed by him and felt that his student had a great future, on completion of his studies Narayanan told his teacher that he could not look forward to much in life in India as he belonged to an untouchable caste. Laski, who had also earned the reputation of being "untouchable" because of his socialist and communist leanings, asked his student not to get disheartened. Prof. Laski wrote a letter to Jawaharlal Nehru praising his student in superlative terms. Nehru was much impressed on reading the letter and invited Narayanan to join the foreign office which he was trying to set up. Thus, Narayanan embarked on a career in diplomacy

Narayanan combined professional diplomacy with scholastic pursuits to produce a new blend of Indian intellectualism in dealing with foreign policy problems. His diplomatic acumen was put to test when in 1976 he was posted as India's Ambassador to Beijing. With his proficiency in Chinese, he began the task of improving the relations with a country which had fought with India in 1962. He served as the Indian Ambassador to Thailand, Turkey, Japan, Britain, Australia and Vietnam. While in Burma (now, Myanmar) he married Ma Tin Tin, a Burmese student, who later adopted the Indian name Usha. Tin Tin, which in Burmese means grace, was a brilliant student of economics in the Rangoon University. The bar on diplomatic service officials marrying foreign nationals was waived at the intervention of Jawaharlal Nehru. Usha Narayanan then had a Masters Degree from the Delhi School of Social Work of the University of Delhi and her field of specialization had been Juvenile Delinquency. She had been closely involved in social welfare activities for women and children. As National President of Karuna, an all-India organization for the welfare of women and children, from 1985 to 1992, she was responsible for building Working Girls' Hostels and Day Care Centres, Potters' Cooperatives and Sericulture projects in Kerala. She had been actively associated with women's organizations in India. In addition to her interest in landscaping, gardening, orchid cultivation, Ikebana and Bonsai, Usha Narayanan also translated Burmese short stories into English. Most of them have been published in the national fortnightly journal, *Frontline*. A collection of her translations of Thein Pe Myint's Burmese Short Stories was published as a book entitled *Sweet and Sour* in December 1998. She also worked with All India Radio for many years, translating and broadcasting news and talks for the External Services of All India Radio. Narayanans had two daughters: Chitra and Amrita.

In 1978, Narayanan retired from the foreign service and was appointed Vice-Chancellor of the Jawaharlal Nehru University. In 1980, Prime Minister Indira Gandhi appointed him Ambassador to Washington, a post he held for four years. After completing this assignment in 1984 he returned home and joined politics and successfully contested the Ottapalam Lok Sabha seat in Kerala, his home state, on the Congress (I) ticket.

Narayanan was chosen the Congress candidate for Ottapalam where the Communist Party of India (Marxist) traditionally had tremendous support. Congress leaders in the State perhaps thought that Narayanan would find it difficult to win from Ottapalam in the erstwhile Malabar. But Narayanan accepted the challenge and won not only the 1984 election but even the two subsequent elections as well. The CPI (M) fielded strong candidates on all the occasions, yet Narayanan won with impressive margins. He was sensitive to the socio-political and economic theories of Mahatma Gandhi as well as Marx. Like Jawaharlal Nehru, whom he greatly admired, Narayanan was a practical Gandhian who acknowledged the positive features of Marxism. After landslide victory of Congress, he was inducted in Rajiv Gandhi's Cabinet and successfully held the portfolios of Planning, External Affairs and Science and Technology.

Narayanan was elected Vice-President in 1992 without any contest. Parties swearing by the social justice plank found in him a person of the appropriate background who would bring honour to the position. The Left parties found in him a person who would restore the traditional axioms of Indian life and foreign policy to the central position from which they were being displaced. Other parties that might have been lukewarm towards him knew that they could not oppose a man of his impeccable credentials without incurring the political cost.

As Vice-President what endeared him to the people was his measured response to any situation and his sober nature. He never took any decision in haste. This attribute, as much as the fact that he had been unflappable even in difficult circumstances, earned him respect and admiration. He was not reported to be running after gods, godmen, astrologers or soothsayers. Nor, as Vice-President, his tour programmes were ever planned in such a way as to include places of worship.

Narayanan had been a member of Indian delegations to the United Nations General Assembly in 1979, to the U.N Security Council in November 1985 on Namibian Independence, to the Conference of Non-Aligned Nations at Harare in 1986, and to the Special Session of the U.N. General

Assembly in May 1986 on the critical situation in Africa. He had been associated with several institutions in diverse capacities. He was President, Indian Council for Cultural Relations; President, Indian Institute of Public Administration; President, Ramakrishna Mission Institute of Cultures, Calcutta (now, Kolkatta); Patron of the International Award for Young People – India. He had been the Chairman of the Jury of the Jawaharlal Nehru Award for International Understanding, the International Jury for Indira Gandhi Prize for Peace, Disarmament and Development; the Advisory Committee for the Rajiv Gandhi Sadbhavana Award; the Jury for International Gandhi Award for Leprosy; the Jury for Indira Gandhi Paryavaran Puraskar; the Jury for Dr B.R. Ambedkar Award for Social Understanding and Upliftment of Weaker Sections; the Jury for Dr B.R. Ambedkar International Award for Social Change; the Jury for G.D. Birla Awards for Humanism, India's Heritage and Culture and Rural Upliftment; and the Jury for Communal Harmony Awards.

A scholar and writer, Narayanan was the author of three books: (1) *India and America: Essays in Understanding*, (2) *Images and Insights*, (3) *Non-Alignment in Contemporary International Relations* (joint authorship). He also contributed a number of articles on social, political, international and literary matters in various magazines and periodicals.

Narayanan was a member of the Universal Academy of Cultures. He was Honorary Fellow of London School of Economics; Honorary Fellow of Jawaharlal Nehru Centre for Advanced Scientific Research, Bangalore, and Honorary Fellow of Centre for Development Studies in Kerala. He was awarded the Jawaharlal Nehru Fellowship in 1970-72 for the Study of Pandit Nehru's Non-Alignment. In 1998, he received the World Statesman Award of the Appeal of Conscience Foundation, New York. He has also received several degrees and honours. They are: Doctor of Science (*Honoris Causa*), University of Toledo, USA; Doctor of Laws (*Honoris Causa*) from the Australian National University. Australian National University has instituted an annual *K.R. Narayanan Oration*. He had been Honorary Professor in Bishkek Humanities

University (Kyrghyz Republic). Sampurnanand Sanskrit University in Varanasi conferred on him *Vachaspati* (D. Litt), the University of San Marcos in Peru the Doctorate (*Honoris Causa*), Tribhuvan University in Nepal conferred on him the Doctorate of Letters (*Honoris Causa*), and the Bilkent University, Turkey, conferred on him the Doctorate of Political Science (*Honoris Causa*). He was the Visitor of Delhi University, Jawaharlal Nehru University and several other central universities. He had also been the Chancellor of Delhi University, Punjab University, Pondicherry University, Assam University, North Eastern Hill University and Gandhigram Rural Institute (Deemed University), Makhanlal Chaturvedi National University Institute of Journalism in Bhopal, and Madras School of Economics.

President K.R. Narayanan retired on July 15, 2002 after completing his full term. Though the Congress Party wanted him to continue for second term but the ruling National Democratic Alliance was not in its favour. He was succeeded by Dr A.P.J. Abdul Kalam, the Defence Scientist. During his presidency Narayanan believed that it is impossible to ensure the country's unity, stability and progress unless the problems of the oppressed castes are solved. He once recalled Ambedkar's statement in this context: "In one of his speeches in the Constituent Assembly, Dr Ambedkar referred to the contradictions between the democracy enshrined in our Constitution and the social and economic inequalities prevailing in our society and said with characteristic asperity that unless these contradictions were resolved, democracy in India will be like a palace built on cow-dung. The foundation may be sacred but feeble and shaky". To this, President Narayanan added: "I would assert that to try to establish democracy or socialism in our country in the real sense, without attacking the caste system, is to pursue a chimera."

Immediately after Narayanan took over, many significant events took place. Laloo Prasad resigned and his wife Rabri Devi was installed as the Chief Minister, Parliament re-enacted 'Freedom at Midnight', Parliament began special four day session to discuss development strategy for the next century, Election Commission of India barred convicts from contesting polls notwithstanding a pending appeal in a higher court, Jain Commission submitted its 17-volume interim report, the Delhi High Court cancelled allotment of petrol pumps by Satish Sharma under Minister's discretionary powers, India fought a successful war with Pakistan in Kargil and the country conducted three nuclear tests in Pokhran range of Rajasthan.

Thus, during his tenure, the Indian political system had been in the throes of cataclysmic changes, posing newer challenges to the office of the President of India. He faced the unenviable task of handling such political developments and handled each of the political exigencies with quite confidence. In March 1998, no party or pre-election alliance of parties had won the number of seats required to give it a clear majority in Lok Sabha and the BJP had emerged as the single largest party, though short of a total majority. The BJP-led pre-election combination of parties and individuals was also the single largest of such formation in the Lok Sabha.

Keeping this in view and to ensure reasonable stability he still explored all other options. He even waited for the letter of support from the AIADMK's suprimo Jayalalitha even if it delayed the swearing-in-ceremony of the new team. His refusal to the BJP-led coalition at the Centre's recommendation on September 22, 1998 for the dismissal of Rabri Devi government in Bihar signaled the warning that a suave-looking, soft-spoken President with a smile writ large on his face cannot be construed to be a mere rubber-stamp in the hands of the Executive.

Above all, President Narayanan's contribution had been conspicuous in three areas. He raised his powerful voice against outbursts of communalism, especially when sections of the ruling elite or State agencies appeared involved. He cautioned against attempts to tinker with the institutions of parliamentary democracy, and spoke for the cause of social justice. In external relations, he played notable role in putting India's relations with China back on the rails. His emphasis on the elimination of slavish mentality was obvious from his address at the banquet hosted for President Clinton in March 2000. While commending politely but clearly the relevance of the non-aligned concept of a pluralistic world order as against the politics of military blocs and alignments as well as on the importance of a multi-polar world, he quoted an African statesman's words that the world, a global village now, doesn't necessarily have to be run by one headman. When the places of worship for Christians were targeted over three years ago by elements known to enjoy the patronage of the people in power, he made use of the New Year message to call upon the people to make 1999 "a year of peace, amity and happiness". Later, the killing in Orissa of Graham Staines and his two young sons evoked severe indictment.

President Narayanan was fully conscious of his constructive role as an elder statesman. When the State of Jammu & Kashmir returned to normalcy after it was severely afflicted with militancy for about a decade to boost the morale of the people he visited the State in November 1997. In his address at the Convocation of the University of Kashmir on November 15, 1997 he hailed the return of normalcy to the troubled valley while laying emphasis on the goals of reconstruction and reconciliation. He held his audience spellbound when he recited two poems by renowned Kashmiri poet Peerzada Ghulam Ahmed Manjoor. As he recited the poem, the audience joined in the penultimate line of each poem and broke into a thunderous applause for President's efforts. His decision to hand out the awards himself added an extra touch of endearment that visibly elated both the students and the faculty members. Later, he denounced the attacks on Christians in some parts of India. In his address to the nation on the eve of Republic Day in 1999, he said that the tradition of tolerance was "at once a pragmatic concept of living together and a philosophic concept of finding truth and goodness in every religion. "

Following the defeat of the BJP-led government in the third week of April 1999 when the opposition managed to muster 270 votes in cliff hanger in the Lok Sabha and getting letters of support from all parties had proved to be a difficult proposition, President Narayanan invited all the opposition parties. When no solution seemed in sight, acting on the past precedents he asked Prime Minister Vajpayee to recommend dissolution of the 12th Lok Sabha. The Vajpayee Cabinet was asked to look after the affairs of the Government till a new House was elected. He had cordial relations with Prime Minister Vajpayee.

Though Narayanan had not been a great orator but his speeches were characterized with logical conclusion. Before making a speech he studied the subject, collected material, mostly from his archives, and talked to experts on the subject. He had been a Nehru scholar and he used to write poetry during his college days. His qualities of a scholar, poet, teacher and a statesman made his speeches coherent, rich in content, placid in presentation and delightful to hear. To listen to him was at once an informative and educative experience, whether he spoke about Bismillah Khan, Semmangudi, the Comprehensive Test Ban Treaty (CTBT), the Dunkel proposals or the current political international situation. His style had been vivid and sharp. While speaking at a function to honour the *shehnai* maestro Ustad Bismillah Khan, Narayanan said: "It has been said that music finds its way where the Sun cannot penetrate. Khan Sahib's music has found its way, penetrating barriers of religion, caste and class, to the hearts of millions of our people, uniting them in a shared ecstasy...He has never accepted that there is any contradiction between music and his religious faith, rather he sees perfect unity, a divine connection between the two..."

Narayanan assumed office of the President of India at a time when the country's politics had been in a state of turmoil. Fortunately, his election was remarkably smooth. The nation's democratic policy had just entered a phase of coalition politics where fractured mandate became the rule rather than an exception and the party system seemed to be on the brink of collapse. But his working relationship with Prime Minister was not disturbed. The presidency was not subjected to any strains though President Narayanan and Prime Minister Vajpayee had different ideological orientations.This brought a qualitative change in the role assigned to the President under the Constitution. After the end of his tenure, we find that the image of the President was no longer that of a figurehead. He was called upon to intervene decisively. T.N Seshan was perhaps right when he said that the need of the hour is not "a rubber stamp President". Narayanan established that President's office is neither wholly ornamental nor activist. It has been a confluence of wisdom and consensus.

K. R. Narayanan expired on November 9, 2005 at the Army Research and Referral Hospital, New Delhi, after being briefly ill with pneumonia and consequent renal failure. He was cremated with full state honours at sunset the following day; the last rites were performed by his nephew Dr P.V. Ramachandran, at *Ekta Sthal* on the banks of the River Yamuna, adjacent to *Shanti Van*, the memorial of his mentor Jawaharlal Nehru.

17

A.P.J. Abdul Kalam

Tenure as President
25 July 2002-25 July-2007
Votes Secured: 992,884
Nearest Rival
Lakshmi Sahgal
Votes Secured: 107,366

1931–

India's eleventh President Dr A.P.J. Abdul Kalam to occupy the office in July 2002 is the father of country's indigenous missile programme. For all his commitment and integrity, unlike his predecessors Dr Abdul Kalam was politically naive, obviously because throughout his life he had been a scientist and technocrat. But he has a vision to transform India into a developed nation by 2020. From a small town of Rameshwaram to Rashtrapati Bhavan his own life had been the story of rise from obscurity and his personal and professional struggles, synonymous with the development of *Prithvi, Akash, Trishul, Nag* and *Agni* missiles that have become household names in India. It was for the first time in the year 2002 that the nation chose a defence scientist to the highest post of the President of India. A man of distinction, a member of a minority community and, most important, an icon with the assertive middle classes, Dr A.P.J. Abdul Kalam has an uncanny inclination to prove everything, rather logically with a unique style of presenting his views in their right perspective. His pragmatic approach to life is summed up in his following poem:

God has not promised skies always blue,
Flower-strewn pathways, all our life through,
God has not promised, Sun without rain,
Joy without sorrow, peace without pain.

Born on October 15, 1931 at Dhanushkodi in a middle class Tamil family in an island town of Rameshwaram district of Tamil Nadu of South India, Avul Pakir Jainulabdeen Abdul Kálam is the son of Jainulabdeen—a little educated boat owner—and Ashiamma, a devout Muslim. His father used to rent boats to fishermen. The boy learnt from his father that there exists a divine power that can lift one up from confusion, misery, melancholy and failure and can guide a person to his place.

Abdul Kalam began his life by selling tamarind seeds to a provision shop which daily fetched him a "princely" sum of one *anna* (a fraction of Indian rupee in pre-partitioned India). He was also helping his cousin to sell the Tamil newspaper, *Dinamani*. He was 6-years old when his father embarked on the project of building a wooden sailboat to take pilgrims from Rameshwaram to Dhanuskodi and back. He watched the boat taking a shape. The wooden hull and bullheads were seasoned with heat from wooden fires. One day, a cyclone took away the boat. A bridge also collapsed with a train full of passengers in it. Till then, the boy had only seen the beauty of the sea. Now, he saw its uncontrollable energy. As a child, the mysteries of the sky and the flight of the birds fascinated him. He used to watch cranes and seagulls soar into flight and longed to fly.

When Abdul Kalam was 10-years old, his teacher, Subramaniam Iyer, told the class how seagulls fly. Abdul Kalam had some doubts and the teacher offered some clarifications. The teacher took the students to the seaside and showed them the birds, explaining every movement and every action. Abdul Kalam listened attentively to the teacher. He learnt from the teacher the purpose in life—to fly.

Abdul Kalam studied in Schwartz High School, a missionary institute, in Ramanathapuram. He was brought up in an atmosphere where the Hindus and Muslims lived and worked together with perfect harmony. Once, when Abdul Kalam was in fourth standard, a mathematics teacher was teaching another class. Inadvertently, Abdul Kalam wandered into that class room when the teacher saw him. He caught the boy by his neck and caned him in front of the whole class. Many months later, Abdul Kalam scored full marks in mathematics. The teacher was surprised. In 1950, Abdul Kalam joined St. Joseph's College in Tiruchirapalli (now Trichi) to pursue intermediate. He graduated from this College with Bachelor of Science. He was not a bright student in terms of examination grade but acquired a practical bent of mind. While in College, Abdul Kalam also developed a taste for classics in English literature. He read Tolstoy, Scott and Hardy. Here he also developed a great interest in Physics and radioactive decay of substance.

For Abdul Kalam, science has always been the path to spiritual enrichment and self-realization. He became an avid reader of books in cosmology and enjoyed reading about celestial bodies. After completing his B.Sc. he joined the Madras Institute of Technology (MIT) which was regarded as the crown jewel of technical education in South India at that time. Education in MIT was quite costly. His father couldn't afford it. His sister Zohra mortgaged her bangles to collect money required for his education. Abdul Kalam, in turn, vowed to release her bangles from mortgage with his own earnings. He studied hard and got a scholarship. Abdul Kalam's association with MIT helped him in his further career. It is there that he started his career for technology development as a team effort. His Professor of Aeronautical Design and Structure, K.A.V. Pandalai, had asked him and four others to design a low-level attack aircraft. "That was a fantastic experience at a young age", Abdul Kalam recalled in an interview, "and that was the foundation." The ability to put heads together and develop things jointly is what Abdul Kalam has carried with him since then, whether it was the design of a hovercraft at the Aeronautical Development Establishment (ADE), or the development of the technology of fibre-reinforced plastic (FRP) at the Thumba Equatorial Rocket Launching Station (TERLS) or building the satellite launch vehicle (SLV) at ISRO or *Agni* under the Integrated Guided Missile Programme (IGMDP). His ability to bring people together and integrate efforts towards a mission made him an excellent team leader and an able project manager, just what a strategic programme like the IGMDP required, with five different systems and associated technologies to be developed.

Abdul Kalam made significant contributions as Project Director to develop India's first indigenous Satellite Launch Vehicle (SLV-III), which successfully injected the Rohini satellite in the near earth orbit in July 1980 and made India an exclusive member of Space Club. He was responsible for the evolution of ISRO's launch vehicle programme, particularly the PSLV configuration. After working for two decades in ISRO and mastering launch vehicle technologies, Abdul Kalam took up the responsibility of developing indigenous Guided Missiles at Defence Research and Development Organization as the Chief Executive of Integrated Guided Missile Development Programme (IGMDP). He was responsible for the development and operationalization of *Agni* and *Prithvi Missiles* and for building indigenous capability in critical technologies through networking of multiple institutions. He was the Scientific Adviser to Defence Minister and Secretary, Department of Defence Research & Development from July 1992 to December 1999. During this period, he led the weaponization of strategic missile systems and the Pokhran-II nuclear tests in collaboration with the Department of Atomic Energy, which made India a nuclear weapon state. He also gave thrust to self-reliance in defence systems by progressing multiple development tasks and mission projects, such as Light Combat Aircraft. He was also the Chairman, Ex-officio, of the Scientific Advisory Committee to the Cabinet (SAC-C) and piloted India Millennium Mission 2020.

Abdul Kalam has received honorary doctorates from thirty universities. He is the recipient of three highest civilian honours: the Padma Bhushan (1981), the Padma Vibhushan (1990) and Bharat Ratna (1997). He has refused another honorary doctorate from a University stating that he is satisfied with the ones he has earned with his hard work and determination.

In 2001, Dr Abdul Kalam took up academic pursuit as Professor, Technology & Societal Transformation at Anna University, Chennai, and was involved in teaching and research activities. He took up this assignment again after completing his term as President of India in July 2007. His mission has always been to ignite the young minds for national development by meeting high school students across the country. He has to his credit four books: *Wings of Fire, India 2020: A Vision for the New Millennium, My Journey* and *Ignited Minds: Unleashing the Power Within India*. These books have become household names in India and are favourite books among the Indian nationals abroad. These books have been translated in many Indian languages.

Dr Abdul Kalam was the Bharatiya Janata Party's candidate for the Presidential election in 2002 and was opposed by the Communist parties. At that time, the BJP was the major component of National Democratic Alliance (NDA), which was in power. He was sworn in as country's President on July 25, 2002. He strongly advocated an action plan to develop India into a knowledge superpower and into a developed nation by the year 2020. His views are reflected in his book, *India 2020*. He is credited with the view that India ought to take a more assertive stance in international relations. In his speech delivered in Hyderabad, he said that his first vision is Freedom, second is Development, third is that India must stand up to the world, and thus his *mantra* or gospel for India is: "freedom, development and stand up to the world". His three visions for India are arrived at on the basis of achievements and progress made by India and during his own career as a missile scientist.

President Dr Abdul Kalam asked his countrymen that climbing to the top demands strength, whether it is to the top of Mount Everest or to the top of their career. To live only for some unknown future is superficial. He advised his countrymen that

There are forces in life working for you and against you. One must distinguish the beneficial forces from the malevolent ones and choose correctly between them. As a child of God, I am greater than anything that can happen to me. We should give up and we should not allow the problem to defeat us. Great dreams of great dreamers are always transcended. Be more dedicated to making solid achievements than in running after swift but synthetic happiness....To succeed in your mission, you must have a single-minded devotion to your goal. Man needs his difficulties because they are necessary to enjoy success. You have to dream before your dreams can come true.....God, our Creator, has stored within our minds and personalities, great potential strength and ability. Prayer helps us to tap and develop these powers.

As President of the Republic of India, he spoke everywhere on the issue of development and peace. On the eve of fifty-fifth Republic Day, he asked the political parties to take into account the aspirations of young people who want to live in a developed and corruption-free India while drawing up their manifestoes. In a departure from tradition, he administered a 10-point oath to hundred youth on January 25, 2004 at the time of the recording of his address to the nation.

These points were:

1 I will pursue my education or work with dedication and I will excel in it.
2 from now onwards, I will teach at least ten persons to read and write.
3 I will plant at least ten saplings and shall ensure their growth.
4 I will visit rural and urban areas and wean away at least five persons from addiction and gambling.
5 I will constantly endeavour to remove the pain of my suffering brethren.
6 I will not support any religion, caste or language differentiation.
7 I will be honest and endeavour to make a corruption free society.
8 I will work towards becoming an enlightened citizen and make my family righteous.

9 I will always be a friend of the mentally and physically challenged and will make them feel normal.
10 I will proudly celebrate the success of my country and my people.

He was India's President with a difference. Even at the age of seventy-two he happened to be the first President to have gone to Siachan, the world's highest battlefield, to meet the country's military people guarding our borders. He braved the chill and spent time interacting with the troops. His friendly handshakes lifted the spirits of soldiers in the biting cold at 18,000 feet above sea level. He took stock of the machines and technology deployed to assist soldiers and indicated the need for improvement. He wanted the time for casualty evacuation to be made faster by increasing the number of the made-in-India chopper *'Dhruv'*. He wanted the high-altitude capability of *'Dhruv'* to be improved so that the Air Force does not have to handle several variants. He also wanted the mounting of helicopters and other types of aircraft with advanced technological aids, such as ground penetration radars, to make patrolling safer for *jawans* by detecting crevasses and taking cloud-penetrating photographs. He also mooted the deployment of high-altitude spy planes for reconnaissance operations. Since the most important aspect in mountain warfare is timely reconnaissance, President Kalam wanted these tools to be supplemented with inputs from remote-sensing satellites.

On April 18, 2004, President Dr Abdul Kalam became the first President of India to remind the nation that "in a democracy, an important principle is the equality of every citizen" and that "elections are an occasion when this can be demonstrated visibly." He asked the citizens "to go to the booths and exercise your franchise." He requested all the eligible voters to vote in large numbers.

When, in July 2004, a number of children became the victim of fire in a school in Kumbakonam in Tamil Nadu, he was deeply grieved by the tragedy and wrote a poem, "Poem for the Departed Children of Kumbakonam" in memory of the 91 children who lost their lives:

Oh dear little ones! Oh dear little ones!
From you, parents had glorious dreams!
And you were all immersed in your own dreams,
Yet, Agni engulfed you and all of those dreams
Taking you to Almighty's divine presence.
Usually, departed old parents are buried by sons,
Whereas, Kumbakonam, saw a sad scene!
Crying parents burying their little ones!!
Oh Almighty! Show Your grace on those little ones,
And keep them all in Thy Holiest Presence!!
Oh Almighty! Bless those parents wilting in grief,
To have the strength to bear this great loss.
May Thy compassion and grace pervade all souls,
And bring down the pain and wipe away the tears.
Oh Almighty! Show Your grace on those little ones.

(*Source:* ***The Hindustan Times****, July 22, 2004*)

People wonder how President Dr Abdul Kalam manages to balance his scientific approach with his spiritual beliefs. In an interview, he clarified that when he looked up into the sky, he observed a million stars. One star—the Sun—is enough to keep our whole solar system running. The thought was overwhelming! It made him realize that we are just specks in the universe. It gave him reason to believe that there is something, something where he could turn to, and so he prayed. He felt content that he had been given everything in life, and much more. He didn't feel the need to pray for himself. Yet, he said that he prayed for his nation, for the people of India, for the young minds who would take his country to the great heights.

During his tenure, he gave PowerPoint presentations about his vision to the parliamentarians, 14 state legislatures on the subject as well as to the foreign dignitaries he met when he visited 16 countries during his presidency. In Zurich in 2005, 12 Nobel laureates came to hear him. So impressed was the Swiss Government by his credentials that it declared the day of his visit—May 26—the national science day. In Singapore, when he made a presentation, a former prime minister of the country remarked that he had never seen the head of a nation making a PowerPoint presentation.

On February 19, 2006, he created history by becoming the country's first President to undertake an undersea journey. He boarded the INS Sindhurakshak, a Russian-origin kilo class submarine, from the Visakhapatnam Naval dockyard. The duration of the journey was around three-and-half hours during which he had lunch with the crew members. On June 8, 2006, he created history by becoming the first President to undertake a sortie in a fighter aircraft, a Sukhoi-30 MKII, from Lohegaon (Pune) airbase. At the age of 74, he created a record by becoming the oldest Indian co-pilot to do so. The President donned a G suit before boarding the aircraft. The flight, flown by Wing Commander Ajay Rathore, lasted for 30 minutes flying at a height of six to eight kilometers in the air at a speed of 1500 km/hr.

Leading the life of a bachelor, vegetarian and a teetotaler, President Dr A.P.J Abdul Kalam recites the *Quran* and the *Bhagavad Gita* with equal devotion. He writes poetry in Tamil, and dreams of a strong India. "We must think and act like a nation of a billion people," he said. On the eve of the year 2006, in an interview to Anubha Sawhney, he said; "I will not be presumptuous enough to say that my life can be a model for anybody; but some poor child living in an obscure place in an underprivileged social setting may find a little solace in the way my destiny has been shaped. It could perhaps help such children liberate themselves from the bondage of their illusory backwardness and hopelessness." In the matrix of his success, President Dr Abdul Kalam has not left anything to fate. "When one has orbited around the Sun seventy times, change becomes a necessity.This change must bring with it new thoughts which lead to innovative actions. I know, my imagination will never let me down. Neither will my dreams. Technology can change the future of man. I have seen it happen in my life." This had been the mission of the First Citizen of India who rose from scratch by dint of his hard work and devotion. He should be a source of inspiration to the generations to come. In his own words

I am a well in this great land,
Looking at its millions of boys and girls,
To draw from me,
The inexhaustible divinity,
And spread His grace everywhere...

He laid down his office on July 25, 2007 on the expiry of his term. He didn't want any political process at the Rashtrapati Bhavan. In the absence of a consensus, he did not like to contest for the second term. Well before the expiry of his term, he had already chalked out post-retirement plan and an itinerary that would keep him busy teaching students across the country. From July 26, 2007, he started moving as a visiting professor at five universities: the Anna University in Chennai, the Gandhigram Rural Institute in Madurai, the Indian Institute of Information Technology (IIIT) in Hyderabad, the Nalanda University in Patna and the newly-established Indian Institute of Space Science and Technology in Thiruvananthapuram. He also started writing three more books.

As a President, his record had been undistinguished. Even while handling political issues, early in his presidency, he demonstrated that he was not a novice. He brought with him all the experience he had gathered while serving six prime ministers. He got along well with both Atal Bihari Vajpayee and Manmohan Singh maintaining his independence without becoming an activist President. He was neither an activist nor a rubber stamp President. While he maintained a balance, he also brought with him an agenda for development that he fiercely marketed right through his presidency. He knew that no prime minister or party could complain if he talked of how to make the nation economically developed by 2020. So, he cleverly used that advantage to propagate his message and ideals wherever he went. His main contribution had been the proposal of propagating PURA (Providing Urban Amenities in Rural Areas), a roadmap for bridging the rural-urban divide. For him Bharat and India were inseparable and the key to development lies in bringing them closer. He has also been pushing for a Pan-African e-network connecting 53 countries and the World Knowledge Platform.

In his latest book, *Turning Points*, published in June 2012, Dr Kalam explained that during his tenure in 2004, he was ready to swear in Sonia Gandhi as Prime Minister without the slightest hesitation despite intense lobbying against the Congress chief. This is contrary to the belief that Sonia's decision to renounce the post was dictated by Dr Kalam's reluctance to let her become the PM in view of her foreign origin.

Politics was obviously not his forte, having spent his life earlier in the pursuit of science and technology. He brought with him no political baggage and unlike earlier presidents like Giani Zail Singh and Fakhruddin Ali Ahmed, Dr Abdul Kalam, in his own idealistic and professional way, gave himself the space and time to insulate himself from the political establishment to add value to the office like few had before him. Fakhruddin Ali Ahmed (1974-77) was even roused from his sleep at the dead of night to sign the proclamation declaring Emergency rule by Prime Minister Indira Gandhi on June 25-26, 1975. He didn't even bother to check whether the measure had cabinet approval. All his successors were hardcore politicians with V.V. Giri and N. Sanjeeva Reddy playing a factional role in the break-up of the Congress. Reddy was sidelined by Indira Gandhi for his role in splitting the party but had his revenge when she lost the 1977 elections and her opponents, led by Morarji Desai, won famously and installed Reddy as President. His successor, Giani Zail Singh took presidential intervention to new heights. In contrast, Dr Abdul Kalam, a non-politician, brought the much-needed dignity and stature to the presidency, his unprecedented popularity among the masses being ample evidence. Unlike some of his predecessors, Dr Abdul Kalam never had hangers-on people or even relatives staying with him in his sprawling mansion. It is learnt that during his tenure he paid for every single relative who was invited to stay with him. In this way, he set the moral agenda for the nation.

Dr Abdul Kalam was accused by some people that during his tenure he kept pending for more than six months Afzal Guru's mercy petition. Though he never said that he didn't get the file, but, in his last interview as President to *India*

Today's Managing Editor Raj Chengappa he said, "If the papers had come to me, I would have processed them for their worth. Before the Government sends me papers of this nature, it has to go through several processes; it has to check with the Cabinet and also the state government concerned. It is going through that process."

One of the major issues that came up during his presidency was the issue of reservation for OBCS in educational institutions and also for the Muslim community. He believed that we have to make the whole reservation issue irrelevant by increasing the number of seats in our colleges, just like engineering colleges which have 20,000 to 30,000 seats. In other areas like bio-science, medicine, management and many specialized fields, we have to add more seats.

During his presidency, attitudes changed in the Rashtrapati Bhavan. Protocol was reduced. The President's staffers were free to call upon him whenever they had to discuss one or more issues. "If you can pick up the phone and speak, why can't you meet me in person", Dr Abdul Kalam used to ask his officials. He told his support team that hierarchy was irrelevant in the new world of communication systems. He would dial mobile numbers of his aids directly without going through the telephone operator.

However, the biggest blot on his tenure was the dissolution of the Bihar Assembly in May 2005 when he acted on the advice of the Centre, a move that was widely condemned and even declared unconstitutional by the Supreme Court.

The facts are like this: Bihar Legislative Assembly comprises of 243 members and to secure an absolute majority support of 122 Members of Legislative Assembly (MLAs) is required. National Democratic Alliance (NDA), a political coalition of parties comprising of the Bharatiya Janata Party (BJP) and the Janata Dal (United), i.e. JD(U), was the largest pre-poll combination having the support of 92 MLAs. The party-wise strength in the Assembly was: NDA 92, RJD 75, LJP 29, Congress (I) 10, CPI(M) 7, Samajwadi Party 4, NCP 3, Bahujan Samaj Party 2, Independents 17, and others 9. On March 6, 2005, the Governor of Bihar sent report to the President of India recommending 'newly-constituted Assembly' to be kept in suspended animation for the present, without summoning the Assembly for the purpose of getting oath of successful members under Article 188 & Para VII A & B. In his report, the Governor apprehended 'horse trading'. The report of the Governor was received by Union of India on May 22, 2005 and, on the same day, the Union Cabinet met at about 11 pm, and decided to accept the report of the Governor and sent a fax message to the President of India, who had already left for Moscow, recommending the dissolution of the Legislative Assembly of Bihar. The President received the message at his Camp office in Moscow at 0152 hrs (IST). The President accorded his approval and sent the same through the fax message, which was received at 0350 hrs (IST) on May 23, 2005.

The case was referred to the Supreme Court in *Rameshwar Prasad & Ors* vs *Union of India* in Writ Petition No.257 of 2005. The first point taken up by the Hon'ble Court was whether it is permissible to dissolve the Legislative Assembly under Article 174 (2)(b) of the Constitution without its first meeting taking place. Article 174 of the Constitution deals with the power of the Governor to summon the House, prorogue the House and dissolve the Legislative Assembly. According to Section 73 of the R.P. Act, the Election Commission must publish results of elections to the Lok Sabha and State Assemblies in the official gazette as declared by the Returning Officers in the State. After a notification in the official gazette is issued Parliament or the Assembly shall be 'deemed' to be constituted. The word 'deemed' is an enabling provision to enable the Governor to summon the House for the purpose of administering the oath of office to the elected candidates so that they can become MLAs to conduct the legislative business. Before the oath, the Governor has no jurisdiction over the successful candidates. He cannot cancel their elections and thereafter declare their seats as vacant requiring fresh election.

But Dr Abdul Kalam's defence is that even though he was in Russia at that time, he had discussions with Prime Minister Manmohan Singh and had the relevant documents transmitted to him electronically before he took the decision. But the issue proved a setback to his image of an impartial constitutional head. He did try to correct that impression by locking horns with the Government on the Office of Profit Bill but achieved what he wanted.

However, as he said in his last interview to *India Today*, he is concerned about the quality of political discourse in the country. It is not being given the highest priority in all political decisions. For instance, no political party has defined which year India would become economically developed. Nor have they discussed how competitive India should be compared to other countries. He himself defined in Parliament that politics is equal to political politics plus development politics. He believed that every political leader—legislator and parliamentarian—has to spend at least 70 per cent on developmental politics. He wanted the electorate to choose leaders on the basis of their developmental track record. As he has stated in his book, *Turning Point: A Journey Through Challenges*, published in June 2012, the verdict of the apex court hurt him and he wanted to quit. But the Prime Minister requested him not to do so.

Dr Abdul Kalam spent five years in office redefining the office of the President of India giving advise, "igniting minds", throwing open those forbidding doors to a cross section of India, mostly ordinary citizens. He once invited 6,000 farmers, another time he played host to 250 policemen from all over India, and also invited postmen and village *sarpanches*. But those he enjoyed playing host to were people with problems who needed his help, those who promise and have talents, and, of course, students from all over the country who were spellbound while he lectured on what they could contribute to the country and his vision for 2020. According to the former Attorney-General Soli Sorbajee, "He has been one of the finest and certainly the best-loved and most-respected presidents." He gave a new vision of accountability to the highest office of the country. Within 24 hours of e-mailing to him, one could get a reply. His universal appeal became evident when he converted his farewell telecast to the nation into a stirring "I have a dream" address that lay down forcefully his 10-point vision of India in 2020.

Dr Abdul Kalam was known as the People's President. He stressed the need to empower all citizens and provide them a good quality of life. He outlined his vision of transforming India into a developed nation before 2020 and suggested how different sections of society could accelerate the process of bringing prosperity to a billion Indians. He wanted the youth population, constituting more than half of our population, to play key roles in many areas by the year 2020. For that purpose, they have to excel themselves in whatever task they do. To inculcate the right values among the children, teachers and parents have to equip themselves and become mentors through their own personal example. Media, with its outreach, he said, can propagate national successes particularly those emanating from rural areas which will act as a great motivator and will also help in spreading the islands of successes to similarly placed regions in the country. He wants every constituent of the government system and corporate sector and the citizens of the nation to contribute for realizing the mission of developed India. He has been reminding lawyers, judges and corporate sector of their constructive role. He asks the religious leaders to work for bringing unity of minds in the country. He once said, every religion has got a spiritual component; it has to establish a bridge through love and compassion. He wants a movement to start. He wants the religious leaders to pave the way for community amity and peace.

President A.P.J. Abdul Kalam, when he took over, was ranked outside politics, widely expected to be at a loss in the chaos of coalition politics. But, at the end of his term, he left a distinctive mark on the presidency. His predecessors were men of formidable stature but Dr Abdul Kalam turned out to be people's President who opened the doors of the Rashtrapati Bhavan to children and others. As people's President, he showed that the post can be a platform for inspiration and progressive leadership. Through his legacy he has left crucial lessons to his successors. Besides that he was a superb communicator. He realized that he could use his office to talk about issues outside politics that were important to India. He spoke in great depth and detail about how India could become a world power and be economically developed by the year 2020. His innate feelings are reflected in the poem he recited to the staff of Rashtrapati Bhavan when he bade them good adieu on the completion of his term.

Mein nirantar chada, chadta raha,
Shikhar kahan hai mere ishwar?
Mein nirantar khojta raha, khojta raha,
Gyan ka bhandar kahan hai mere ishwar?
Mein nav kheta raha, kheta raha,
Shanti ka dweep kahan hai mere ishwar?
He ishwar, mere desh ko doordrishti aur mehnat se anand prapti ka vardan do.

When translated from Hindi to English, it means: I have climbed relentlessly, where is the summit my lord? I have searched relentlessly, where is the fountain of wisdom my lord? I kept rowing the boat, where is the island of peace my lord? My lord, allow my country to attain happiness through farsightedness and hard work.

18
Pratibha Devisingh Patil

Tenure as President
25 July 2007-25 July 2012
Votes Secured: 638,116
Nearest Rival
Bhairon Singh Shekhawat
Votes Secured: 331,306

1934 –

At a time when the movement for the empowerment of women has gained momentum, in 2007 Pratibha Devisingh Patil became the first President in Independent India. She thus joined the galaxy of women presidents the world over: Dalia Itzik in Israel, Ellen Johnson-Sirleaf in Liberia, Gloria Macapagal-Arroyo I in Philippines, Mary McAleese in Ireland, Micheline Calmy-Rey in Switzerland, Michelle Bachelet in Chile, Tarja Halonen in Finland and Dr Vaira Vilie-Freiberga in Latvia. In Asia, the women who then occupied this enviable post had been: Chandrika Kumaratunge in Sri Lanka (1994-2005), Corazon Aquino in Philippines (1986-1992). Gloria Macapagal-Arroyo I in Philippines, Megawati Sukarnoputri in Indonesia (2001-2004), and Sukhbaatarju Yanjmaa in Mongolia (1953-1954). However, other heads of states, though not designated as such, have been: The Queen of the United Kingdom Elizabeth II, Angela Merkel (Chancellor of Germany), Michaelle Jean (Governor-General, Canada), and Queen of the Netherlands H.M. Beatrix.

Pratibha is the daughter of Narayan Paglu Rao in Nadgaon in Maharashtra. She was born on December 19, 1934. She is the only sister among five brothers. She studied in R.R. School at Jalgaon and obtained her M.A. degree from Mooljee Jaitha

(M.J) College, Jalgaon. Her father wanted her to be a lawyer. But the Principal of the College spotted her talents for interacting with the people and advised her to take up politics as her career. Pratibha, therefore, decided to accede to the wishes of both her elders. She joined the Government Law College, one of the oldest and most distinguished law colleges in India known for preparing legal luminaries like Bal Gangadhar Tilak, Mahadev Govind Ranade, B.R. Ambedkar, Motilal Setalvad and H.M. Seervai. Pratibha was a brilliant student in Law College.

After practicing law for some time, Pratibha began her political career in 1962 at the age of 27 when she wanted to contest her first Assembly election. By this time, her father had come round to her professor's viewpoint. Narayan Rao told his daughter, Pratibha, that he had some money which he saved for her dowry. The option was whether to utilize that money for her dowry or for election. Pratibha too did not want any dowry to be given. "I will not marry a man who wants money from my father," she said. She won the election from Nadgaon and kept winning the polls till 1985.

She met and married Devisingh Ransingh Shekhawat. The Shekhawat family had migrated from Sikar district in Rajasthan to settle in Amravati in Vidharbha. Devisingh was teaching at that time. They were married on July 7, 1965. Devisingh was not in favour of dowry. For him it was a great satisfaction that his wife was highly educated. During those days, it was difficult to get an educated bride. Being active in Maharashtra politics, she preferred not to take her husband's surname. When Pratibha became minister in Maharawshtra in the V.P. Naik cabinet, the couple shifted to Mumbai. The couple has two children. Her son, Rajendra, is now a businessman and daughter, Jyoti, is a software engineer. While Pratibha devoted her life to social activities, the children were brought up by the two widowed *massis* (mother's sisters) steering them to school till Shekhawats moved them to Amravati for higher education.

Pratibha had been quite loyal to the Congress Party and to Indira Gandhi. Under the mentorship of senior Congress leader and ex-Chief Minister Yashwantrao Chavan, she became a deputy minister for education after re-election in 1967 in Vasantrao Naik's cabinet. In her next term, during 1972-78, she was a full Cabinet minister in Maharashtra. From 1972 to 1974 she was a Cabinet Minister looking after Social Welfare. From 1974 to 1975 she had the portfolio of Public Health & Social Welfare in Maharashtra. In 1975-76, she had Prohibition, Rehabilitation and Cultural Affairs in the Maharashtra Government. In 1977-78, she was Education Minister in the state. In this way, she handled different portfolios under the chief ministership of Vasantdada Patil, Babasaheb Bhosale, S.B. Chavan and Sharad Pawar. She was continuously re-elected to the Assembly, either from Jalgaon or the nearby Edlabad constituencies.

Following the Emergency and defeat of Indira Gandhi in 1977, the Congress Party was split up in two factions. Many senior leaders of the state Congress (I), including Pratibha's mentor Chavan and his protégé Sharad Pawar and many others joined the Congress (Urs), the Party floated by Devraj Urs. However, Pratibha preferred to remain with Indira Gandhi. She protested the arrest of Indira Gandhi in December 1977 and spent ten days in prison. In 1978, when the Congress (Urs) came to power in Maharashtra, she became Leader of the Opposition in the State Assembly.

In 1980, when the Congress (I) regained power Pratibha's name was considered as a front-runner for the Chief Minister's post. However, the post went to Sanjay Gandhi's confidant, A.R. Antulay, who was soon forced to resign on corruption changes. Subsequently, she became a minister again in the Vasantdada Patil ministry. Following differences between Patil and then Maharashtra Pradesh Congress Committee (MPCC) Chief Prabha Rau, Rajiv Gandhi appointed her as Chief of the Pradesh Congress Committee.

In 1985, Pratibha was elected to the Rajya Sabha as a Congress candidate. In Rajya Sabha, she was the Deputy Chairperson from 1986 to November 1988. She had also been the Chairperson of the Committee on Privileges. Her term expired in April 1999. The following year, in the 10th Lok Sabha election, she was elected from her husband's constituency Amravati, where he had once been mayor.

Together with her husband, Pratibha set up an educational institute, Vidya Bharati Shikshan Prasarak Mandal, which runs a chain of schools and colleges in Jalgaon and Mumbai. She also set up Shram Sadhana Trust that runs hostels for working women in New Delhi, Mumbai and Pune and an engineering college in Jalgaon. She also founded and had been the Chairperson of a cooperative sugar factory known as Sant Muktabai Sahakari Sakhar Karkhana and a cooperative bank named after herself as Pratibha Mahila Sahakari Bank. She was also involved in the setting up of an Industrial Training School for the visually challenged in Jalgaon. A school was opened for poor children of Vimukta Jamatis and Nomadic Tribes. She served as Director of National Federation of Urban Cooperative Bank & Credit Societies and had been the Member of Governing Council, National Cooperative Union of India.

In November 2004, following the resignation of Madan Lal Khurana, Pratibha Devisingh Patil succeeded him as the first woman Governor of Rajasthan. With Pratibha Devisingh Patil as Governor, Rajasthan had women in three significant positions of power. In addition to Patil herself at the top, they were: Chief Minister Vasundhara Raje and Assembly Speaker Sumitra Singh. During her tenure, in April 2006, the Rajasthan Legislative Assembly passed the Rajasthan Freedom of Religion Bill 2006. The objective of the Bill was to control "unlawful conversion from one religion to another by allurement or by fraudulent means or forcibly." However, some Christian organizations opposed the Bill alleging that the Bill was an outcome of the rightist policies of Sangh Parivar. Pratibha Devisingh Patil returned the Bill unsigned stating that certain clauses in the Bill infringed the "fundamental rights, such as freedom of speech and expression, freedom of conscience and freedom to profess, practice and propagate religion." The Government of Rajasthan re-sent the Bill to her in May 2006 noting that similar anti-conversion laws enacted by the Congress governments in Madhya Pradesh and Orissa over 40 years ago were upheld by the Supreme Court of India and that the head of the Constituent Assembly, Dr B.R. Ambedkar, while drafting Article 25 of the Constitution, had said that it would be best to leave it to the

State legislatures to make laws to regulate conversions. After keeping the Bill pending for around a year, Pratibha sent it to the President of India just a day before she resigned as Governor of Rajasthan. She resigned as Governor on June 21, 2007 when she became a presidential candidate.

Pratibha Devisingh Patil was United Progressive Alliance (UPA)-Left candidate for the post of President of India. She faced NDA-supported Bhairon Singh Shekhawat, then the Vice President of India. The Electoral College consisted of 4,472 votes. Of this, 4,394 were the valid votes this time, with a value of 9,69,422. In the proportional representation system of voting, MPs have a uniform value of 708 for each vote, while the value of the vote of a Member of a Legislative Assembly (MLA) differs from State to State. Uttar Pradesh, the most populous State, accounts for the highest value of 208 for each vote and Sikkim the lowest value of seven. She won 3,06,810 (65.82 per cent), getting 6,38,116 votes defeating Bhairon Singh Shekhawat who polled 3,31,306 (33.18 per cent). The break-up is as follows: In Parliament, she had 442 votes against 232 for Shekhawat. With the states and union territories put together, the winning candidate bagged 2489 votes against the loser's 1217.

Pratibha Devisingh Patil also made unexpected gains in Assam, where 15 legislators of the Asom Gana Parishad (AGP), a constituent of the UNPA voted in her favour. In BJP-ruled Madhya Pradesh too, Shekhawat had fewer votes than expected, as about 11 votes were invalidated because they were inscribed with pro-Hindutva slogans such as "Jai Sri Ram". As many as 78 votes were invalid. Shekhawat's connections seem to have worked in only two States: Rajasthan, his home State, where he had the support of four INLD members, and Tamil Nadu, where he got 58 votes from members of the AIADMK and the MDMK. In Madhya Pradesh, some evidence of his connections could be seen as five members of the S.P. voted in his favour. Members of these parties, all constituents of the UNPA, voted for Shekhawat despite the decision of their respective parties to abstain. But these gains were offset by the loss of BJP votes in Gujarat, Madhya Pradesh and Chhattisgarh.

She was sworn in on July 25, 2007. She listed her priorities in her maiden speech. She maintained that "empowerment of women is particularly important" to her as "it leads to the empowerment of the nation". She called for universal education and promised to fight for the vast mass of underprivileged in the country. Honest pursuit of such an agenda should evoke widespread support from across the political spectrum and the masses.

Ever since she took over this highest office in the country, the focus in her speeches had been on the eradication of social evils. In her public speeches and in the suggestions she has made to the political government she has emphasized on the need to overcome poverty, gender inequality, female foeticide, maternal and child malnutrition, and specific social evils. She has dwelt on the economic costs attached to these social deficits. She has offered her reflections on key issues like women's empowerment, expansion of education, agriculture and rural development, national security, and for the need to develop compassion towards the underprivileged.

President Pratibha Patil had been taking a keen interest in the education and training in journalism. She believes that the media can play a significant role in the social transformation. She wants the media to play a constructive role in the eradication of social evils. Since she herself had been involved in social activities at times, she goes into specifics and like a mother teaching or counseling the family members, she had been talking to the whole country as her family to bring in transformation in our society.

She has shown her concern for child marriage which is still prevalent in Rajasthan, Madhya Pradesh and Bihar and, to some extent, in other states as well, where girls are still being married at the age of 10 to 13 years. These girls have their first child just when they attain puberty, sometime even 5 to 6 children by then. In this way, even at a young age they get extremely worried about their children. President Pratibha Patil also showed her concern about the maternal and infant mortality in some parts of India. She feels that our people in this situation can never come out of poverty. She has observed that one child marriage has ten ill effects. She feels that our journalists should primarily be exposed to areas which are the breeding ground of poverty.

Alcohol is the second evil which President Pratibha Patil has advocated for poverty elimination. The eradication of alcohol is a socio-economic challenge. She has emphasized on the need for regular and imaginative schemes to bring alcoholics out of their addiction, which would otherwise ruin them and their families.

The third issue which had been of major concern to the Hon'ble President was women's empowerment and the establishment of a greater gender-just society. She spoke about the pro-women leanings in our constitutional philosophy, the enactment of welfare legislation to protect women and end discrimination against them and their subordinate status in society, their representation in urban and rural bodies, progressive changes in the rules of evidence and legal procedure, and women to compete equality with men in various professions, including law which once used to be the preserve of males. She called upon civil society groups, especially lawyers, to be vigilant so that the legal provisions are implemented effectively and fairly showing sensitiveness towards women. She wanted Pre-Natal Diagnostic Techniques Act, enacted in 1996, to be implemented in an effective way to totally avoid female foeticide.

President Pratibha Patil also voiced her concern against the system of dowry and violence on women. At the same time, she had been pointing out the main points that have led to the improper implementation of anti-dowry laws and other laws concerning women, and those who control the law. She feels that the issues at stake need much more in-depth study and discussion that they seem to have got so far.

On May 25, 2009, President Pratibha Patil made history by taking off in a frontline Sukhoi-30 MKI fighter jet aircraft from the air force base in Pune, becoming the first woman head of state to fly in a warplane. 74-year-old Patil also set a world record by becoming the oldest woman to be airborne in a combat jet for a 30-minute sortie at a speed close to the supersonic level.

Newspapers on March 26, 2012 reported that the President made 12 foreign trips covering 22 countries across four continents. Later, she also visited Seychelles and South Africa.

At the end of her tenure, President Pratibha Patil was criticized by the media for saving murderers, rapists and killers from the hangman. It was reported that no president in India's history has used the power to pardon death-row inmates as extensively as President Patil. She granted a record of 30 pardons in the last 28 months, over 90 per cent of India's total death sentences pardoned ever.

But 22 of these relate to brutal multiple murders and gruesome crimes on children, the worst of which human beings can do to another. Some are rogues who lived on the edge of law and bounced in and out of jails for most of their adult lives. Yet, others have shocked the conscience of the courts by the viciousness of their crimes. Almost every case of clemency in 2012 tells the story of unmitigated brutality against children.

"The philosophy of punishment rests on four tenets," says Markanday Katju, former Supreme Court judge, now Press Council's chairman. "It can be a deterrent work by creating fear. It can be retributive, making one pay for it." It can also be preventive, to stall a crime, or reformative, to strengthen the human character. It's the last theory that inevitably works behind clemency.

As the legendary American jurist, Oliver Wendel Holmes, pointed out, in a modern democracy, the power to punish with death rests with the judiciary and the power to spare life with the executive. "It is for the judiciary to find a person guilty or not and their job ends there," says former Chief Justice of India, Justice J.S. Verma. "Mercy is entirely an executive process for the President to do. Article 72 of the Constitution gives the President absolute and unfettered power to grant pardon, suspend, remit or commute sentences, even in death penalty. But he has to act on the advice of the Union Council of Ministers.

In her farewell speech to Parliamentarians in the Central Hall of Parliament in New Delhi, Pratiba Patil pointed out that varied political thinking is a part of any legislature and more in a country as large and diverse as India. Though this adds to the "vibrancy" of our democratic institutions, it also poses a challenge as a multiplicity of expectations is to be met. "Naturally, there will be arguments in the process of the search for answers, but it should never happen that in the din we loose our way forward. At the end of the day, the worth, value and respect of a legislature is judged by its output in terms of serious debate and legislations," she said.

Pratibha Patil said governments and legislatures need to seriously reflect on the technological changes and our deep thought should be given by Hon'ble Members to how our institutions, our administrative practices, legislatures and legal processes, can fulfill these growing demands and responsibilities effectively.

19

Pranab Mukherjee

Tenure as President
25 July 2012
Votes Secured: 713,763
Nearest Rival
Purno Agitok Sangma
Votes Secured: 315,987

1935–

From village to Rashtrapati Bhavan is the story of Pranab Kumar Mukherjee, a veteran politician. He maintained a low profile in his village. Many people in his village didn't hear much about him except during Durga Puja when he made it a yearly ritual to attend it in his village. He became the first Bengali to be the thirteenth President of Independent India to succeed Pratibha Devisingh Patil in July 2012. Though he is a "Son of Bengal" and has unmistakable Bengali accent, his roots have never been in the state politics; he is a man who has carved for himself a distinct place in the national politics. Annapurna, Pranab Mukherjee's sister, once predicted that her brother would be president one day. This proved prophetic on July 25, 2012 when he was sworn in as the President of India. His name was announced by the Congress President Sonia Gandhi just on the eve of filing of nominations, i.e. on June 15, 2012 after her brief meeting with the UPA partners. It put an end to the long suspense that marked rollercoaster race for the nomination of its presidential candidate by the ruling alliance.

In 2012, if there had been one politician in India who ensured the right to occupy the office through years of distinguished service, it is Pranab Mukherjee. Of course,

Rashtrapati Bhavan's gain had been loss to the Congress Party and the United Progressive Alliance (UPA) Government. For them, the former finance minister had been a man of all seasons. For the Congress Party Mukherjee's long political experience was a real asset. He held almost every important portfolio in government, including defence and foreign affairs, some of them twice. Only the time will tell who can fill up the void so created by him in the Congress so effectively. His sharp political instincts made him a vital asset in an era of fractured and coalition politics. He was the party's and government's bridge with allies.

He is considered to be the chief troubleshooter, master strategist and quintessential Congressman. He has helped the Congress to solve the gravest of crises. "Whenever there is a crisis, he is there. Twenty-five years ago he presented the budget and did so again yesterday as it was a crisis situation. Ever since I was introduced to Pranab Mukherjee I have always appreciated his ability, his strength and his capability to shoulder responsibility", said L.K. Advani, senior BJP leader on February 17, 2009 in Parliament while moving motion of thanks on President's Address. Yet another BJP leader, while speaking in Parliament on October 18, 2011 and while referring to Mukherjee said, "Many leaders in government are smug and arrogant but you can charm even your critics."

Earlier, Sonia Gandhi, it was reported, was reluctant to spare him from the Congress Party 'as he still had much to do'. But it was the general consensus among the UPA's supporting partners that made him the frontrunner. This shows that Mukherjee was considered indispensable in the Congress Party, especially in the coalition scenario when somebody with the necessary skill should reconcile the conflicting parties. But, according to Mukherjee, "Indian democracy has the flexibility to accommodate and absorb difficult situations."

Pranab Kumar was born on December 11, 1935 in a small village, Mirati, in Birbhum District in West Bengal. He is the son of Late Shri Kamada Kinkar Mukherjee and Smt. Rajlakshmi Mukherjee. His father was a respected freedom fighter and an active member of Indian National Congress.

He was President of District Congress Committee, Birbhum in West Bengal and was a member of West Bengal Council from 1952 to 1964. He spent more than 10 years in British jails.

Pranab was educated in Vidyasagar College. His career got off to a humble start when he joined the deputy accountant-general's office in Kolkata. He quit to become a college teacher and later worked as a journalist in the Bengali publication, *Desher Dak* (Call of Motherland). He taught political science at Vidyasagar College in North 24-Parganas. He had his master degree in political science as well as in history. He also holds a degree in law from the University of Calcutta. He became professor in a college in Birbhum District of West Bengal. He has been an advocate and a college teacher in his long public career. In 2011, he was awarded an honorary Doctor of Letters degree by the University of Wolverhampton. He also became trustee of Bangiya Sahitya Parishad and later President of Nikhil Bharat Banga Sahitya Sammelan. In 1997, he was voted as an Outstanding Parliamentarian.

Pranab Kumar was married to Suvra on July 13, 1957. Suvra is known as Geetanjali. He has two sons, Abhijit and Indrajit, and a daughter. He is inspired by Deng Xiaoping and has quoted him quite frequently.

Prime Minister Indira Gandhi handpicked Pranab Mukherjee. Thus began a journey for him into the power echelons of Delhi, a career scripted by dint of hard work and merit. Mukherjee was elected for the first time to the Rajya Sabha in 1969. He started his parliamentary career in this way from Congress Party in 1969. Thereafter, he was re-elected in 1975, 1981, 1993 and 1999. His ministerial career began in February 1973 when he became the Deputy Minister, Industrial Development.

The Congress Party always found a way to send him to Rajya Sabha and inducted him in ministries. He was taken as Minister of State for Finance from October 1974 to December 1975, Minister of Revenue and Banking (independent charge) from December 1975 to March 1977, Cabinet Minister of Commerce and Steel & Mines from January 1980 to January 1982, Cabinet Minister of Finance from January 1982 to

December 1984 with additional charge of the Ministry of Commerce and Supply, from September to December 31, 1984, Deputy Chairman, Planning Commission, June 1991 to May 1996, Cabinet Minister of Commerce from January 1993 to February 1995, Cabinet Minister of External Affairs from February 1995 to May 1996, Cabinet Minister of Defence from May 22, 2004 to October 26, 2006, and Cabinet Minister of Finance from January 24, 2009 till July 20 and after that he contested the election and was sworn in as India's Thirteenth President.

His crisis management skills—be it for the government or the party—contributed in elevating him as one of the most trusted lieutenants of Congress president Sonia Gandhi.

Pranab Mukherjee was a Minister in Indira Gandhi's Cabinet during the infamous Emergency and was held by many to be personally responsible for some of the excesses. He was summoned before the Shah Commission but followed Indira Gandhi's footsteps in refusing to resign before it. A police case was registered against him which was withdrawn when Indira Gandhi returned to power. S, Gurumurthy and Arun Shourie exposed how Pranab Mukherjee, the then Finance Minister of India, helped Reliance Industries against Bombay Dyeing through differential taxation by influencing the Income Tax Department in textile industry. As a result, Bombay Dyeing was almost decimated..

His first term as Finance Minister was noted for India not withdrawing the last billion installment of an IMF loan. Dr Manmohan Singh was then serving the Reserve Bank of India as Governor. He was not included in Rajiv Gandhi's cabinet after Lok Sabha election held subsequent to Indira Gandhi's assassination. He was the President of the West Bengal state unit of Congress since 1985, but resigned in July 2010 due to work-load and was succeeded by Manas Bhunia.

Mukherjee's short eclipse came after Indira's assassination when it was suspected he harboured Prime Minister's ambitions. After a brief stint outside the Congress and forming his own party, Mukherjee returned to the Congress to start regaining his position of a key strategist from scratch. P.V. Narasimha Rao brought him back to the union cabinet and gave him plum posts like commerce minister, foreign minister, deputy chairman of planning commission and shielded him against occasional efforts of Mukherjee's 'well wishers' within the Congress to retire him. Thus, he returned to prominence in 1991 during P.V. Narasimha Rao's rule. Many fondly called him a "living encyclopedia" when he was in the Planning Commission .

Once a group of senior Congressmen explained at length why Pranab Mukherjee should not be made the governor of Uttar Pradesh, a politically crucial state for the Congress. Rao heard them with his trade mark patience and then replied: "Already 90 per cent of our voters have gone to the Samajwadi Party and other parties. If Pranab becomes UP governor, his Hindi skills will force the rest 10 per cent to run away as well.

In fact, Mukherjee is stated to have learnt his political skills from his idol and mentor Indira Gandhi. Even during any private conversation, Mukherjee fondly recalls his memories of the long association with Indira Gandhi that started after she heard one of his speeches in the Rajya Sabha in 1969. Indira Gandhi repeatedly asked him not to contest the 1980 Lok Sabha poll. But keen to shed the perception of being a "rootless worker" he fought and lost. Indira Gandhi called him at his Kolkata residence and told him: "Everyone knew that you will lose. Even Geeta (Mukherjee's wife) knew it. But still you went ahead and created trouble for me". She then hung up without even allowing him to reply. Two days later her son, Sanjay Gandhi, telephoned to him to say "Mummy is very angry with you. But she also said, there can't be any cabinet without Pranab. Take a flight for Delhi tomorrow."

Mukherjee has tremendous admiration for Indira's daughter-in-law, Sonia Gandhi, especially for keeping national interest above anything else and for skilful party management. His return to finance ministry in 2009 was primarily because Sonia Gandhi wanted him there.

A budget was to be presented within a month. Mukherjee wasted no time in meeting the Congress president for guidance. When he asked what all she wanted to see in the budget, Sonia reportedly told the finance minister, "More than economic jargon I know one thing. I am for the poor people of our country. Do something for them." Mukherjee's budget envisaged huge rise in expenses in the social sector schemes.

When there was a need to drop Adarsh–tainted Ashok Chavan as Maharashtra chief minister in 2010, Sonia deputed there Mukherjee along with A.K. Antony, the party in charge for Maharashtra. The two leaders returned to the capital from Mumbai around 3 am. Sonia had been desperately waiting and called the two leaders to immediately meet her.

Pranab Mukherjee had been a member of the Congress Working Committee (the highest policy making body of Indian National Congress from January 27, 1978 to January 18, 1986 and again from August 10, 1997 till date. He became the President of West Bengal Pradesh Congress Committee in 1985 and from August 2000 till 2012, member of Central Parliamentary Board, AICC from 1978 to 1986, Treasurer of the All India Congress Committee from 1978 to 1979, Treasurer of the Congress (I) Party in Parliament from 1978 to 1979, Chairman of the Economic Advisory Cell, AICC, from 1987 to 1989, Chairman of the Campaign Committee of AICC for conducting National Elections to Parliament in 1984, 1991, 1996 and 1998. He had been the General Secretary of AICC for 1998-1999. He had been the Chairman of Central Election Coordination Committee, AICC since June 1999, member of the Central Election Committee, AICC from December 2001.

As External Affairs Minister he was involved in handling Taslima Nasreen's house arrest in Delhi. He dealt with a situation involving her expulsion from Kolkata, anger from Islamic radicals, and her protection in a safe house. It has been reported that it was Mukherjee's political maneuvers which ensured that the nuclear deal went through and the Government stayed alive. Mukherjee was well respected by the Opposition—the JD (U) and Shiv Sena backed him for presidentship. He was the troubleshooter with civil society, represented by Team Anna, when all the other leading lights of the Congress had failed miserably. He was known for taking effective decisions.

Mukherjee was the one troubleshooter who could steer the ship of state. He had been the perennial number two ever since Indira Gandhi gave him that role in 1980, bypassing such stalwarts in her cabinet as R. Venkataraman, N.D. Tiwari, Giani Zail Singh and P.V. Narasimha Rao. The fact that he was prepared to concede ground on merit facilitated his task of hammering out a consensus on crucial issues. Persuasion was his most potent weapon. He could give in readily if he found the opponent convincing. This is the reason why he was fielded by the Congress leaders on most occasions to break logjams in Parliament or outside.

He was criticized for his actions leading to Nasreen's eventual departure from India in March 2008. He has also been accused of threatening banks if they invest in Gujarat by sending the Income Tax Department sleuths after them, a state governed by the Bharatiya Janata Party.

A survey of *Euromoney* magazine rated Mukherjee as the best Finance Minister of the World in 1984. In 2010, *Emerging Markets*, the daily newspaper of record for the World Bank and the International Monetary Fund (IMF) awarded him with the title "Finance Minister of the Year for Asia". In December 2010, *The Banker* recognized him as "Finance Minister of the Year".

In 2004, Pranab Mukherjee was elected to the Lok Sabha for the first time from Jangipur Lok Sabha constituency in West Bengal. When the Congress formed a government as the major party in the United Progressive Alliance (UPA) with Dr Manmohan Singh as the Prime Minister Pranab Mukherjee was made Leader of the House in the Lok Sabha. He was Union Minister of Defence from May 22, 2004 to October 26, 2006. On October 24, 2006 he became the Minister of External Affairs and continued to adorn this portfolio till May 23, 2009 when he became the Minister of Finance till the time of his filing of nomination papers for president's election scheduled on July 19, 2012. As External Minister he successfully signed the Nuclear Non-Proliferation Treaty.

His first stint as the Finance Minister of India was during the Indira Gandhi government in 1982. He presented his first annual budget for 1982-83. In the second government of

Dr Manmohan Singh, he again became the Finance Minister of India. On July 6, 2009, he presented the government's second annual budget. In it, he announced many tax reforms, such as the scrapping of the 'irritant' Fringe Benefits Tax and the Commodities Transaction Tax. He announced that the Finance Ministry was well on track to implement the Goods and Services Tax, a tax that has been praised by major corporate executives and economists. He also expanded funding for social sector schemes, like the National Rural Employment Guarantee Act, a girl's literacy and health care. He expanded infrastructure programmes like the National Highway Development Programme, expansion of electricity coverage, and the Jawaharlal Nehru National Urban Renewal Mission. However, many people expressed concern about the rising fiscal deficit, the highest since 1991. Mukherjee said that the expansion in government spending was only temporary and he said that the government was committed to the principle of fiscal prudence. He presented the 2009, 2010, 2011 and 2012 union budgets of India.

Pranab Mukherjee is very well respected within the Congress party's social circles. Other media accounts describe him as having "a reputation as a number-crunching politician with a phenomenal memory and an unerring survival instinct." After Sonia Gandhi reluctantly agreed to join politics, Mukherjee was one of her key mentors, guiding her through difficult situations with examples of how her mother-in-law, Indira Gandhi, would have done things. His unfailing loyalty and competence have led to his closeness to Sonia Gandhi and Manmohan Singh, and helped him gain the position of Minister of Defence when the party came to power in 2004.

His talents were on display during the negotiations for the Patent's Amendment Bill in early 2005. The Congress was committed to pass the IP bill, but the allies of UPA from the Left Front had a long tradition of opposing some of the monopoly aspects of intellectual property. Pranab Mukherjee, as Defence Minister, was not formally involved but was roped in for his skills in negotiation. He drew on many old alliances including the CPI-M leader Jyoti Basu, and formed new intermediary positions, which included product patent and little else. Then he had to convince his own colleagues including commerce minister, Kamal Nath, at one point saying, "An imperfect legislation is better than no legislation." Finally, the bill was approved on March 23, 2005.

Pranab Mukherjee had been a member of the Business Advisory Committee, Committee on Privileges, Committee on Rules, Consultative Committee for External Affairs 1996-1999. He was the Chairman of the Department related Parliamentary Standing Committee on Science & Technology, Environment & Forests 1997, Chairman of the Department-related Parliamentary Standing Committee on Home Affairs June 1998 onwards, Leader of the House, Lok Sabha, June 2004 till July 2012.

He headed 15 of the 27 GoMS, and all but one of the Empowered GoMS. Between UPA 1 and 2, he chaired around 85 GoMS. The areas covered by them ranged from issues as diverse as spectrum pricing, ultra mega project, mass rapid transport system policy and price band of shares held by the Government in PSU.

His leadership in the Ministry of Finance and other economic ministries was well acclaimed, nationally and internationally. He was considered Number 2 in the Cabinet and as the key figure in formulating economic policies of the nation for a long term. Under his stewardship India earned the distinction of not withdrawing the last installment of IMF loan to the extent of US$1.1 billion. He was considered Number 2, as ranking minister, presided over the Cabinet meeting of the Union in the absence of the Prime Minister during 1980-1985.

He had been the member of the Board of Governors of International Monetary Fund (1982-1985), of the World Bank (1982-1985), Asian Development Bank (1982-1985), African Development Bank (1982-1985), Chairman of the Group 24 (a ministerial group attached to IMF and World Bank) in 1984, and presided over SAARC Council of Ministers Conference in May 1995 and November 1995.

He is an author of five books: *Midterm Poll* (1969), *Beyond Survival: Emerging Dimensions of Indian Economy* (1984), *Off the Track* (1987), *Saga of Struggle and Sacrifice* (1992), and *Challenges Before the Nation* (1992).

In his entire life, Mukherjee has seen two movies so far. The last one was Aamir Khan's *Rang De Basanti*. He was then the defence minister and the censor board wanted his approval. He took the three service chiefs to the theatre and told Sharmila Tagore who then was the censor board chief, that she was outsourcing her job to him, as reported in *The Hindustan Times*.

Dr Pranab Mukherjee's heroes are Jawaharlal Nehru and Mahatma Gandhi. But his greatest admiration is for Indira Gandhi. As he told *India Today* in an interview, he has read almost every speech of Jawaharlal Nehru, who made every effort to build the country to take it forward. He is a voracious reader. His range of reading is amazing. Some years ago, there was uproar in Parliament about textbooks that claimed Hindu deities drank alcohol. Mukherjee replied to debate saying this was true. He fluently quoted Chandi Mangal, the traditional Bengali narrative of the battle between Durga and Mahishasura. His links with academia always remained strong. Till recently, he was associated with the Indian Statistical Institute, Rabindra Bharti University and Asiatic University. His favourite book is said to be *Arthashastra*.

Throughout his life, President Mukherjee had been a workaholic. He mostly worked for 10-15 hours in the office, particularly as Finance Minister of India. He is a religious man. He is particular about his daily *puja*. One could find him sparing four days from his busy schedule every year for Durga Puja in his ancestral home Mirati, Birbhum District in West Bengal. It is to be seen whether the President shall continue to perform his *Puja* in his ancestral home or in Rashtrapati Bhavan in the days to come..

It is believed that President Mukherjee is not likely to be a rubber stamp president. Once he said, "If I am elected president, a new era would start for me after nearly four decades in politics. For the president, there is neither politics nor any party; he acts according to the Constitution." There are challenges ahead of him. The next general election in 2014 is not likely to support one party with an overwhelming majority. The coalition politics is likely to take a sharp turn. But for 'Chanakya in Indian politics', as he was referred to in Parliament, is sure to brave through this storm with great equanimity. President Mukherjee is conscious of this. During his campaign in Agartala, he said, "Though the President is virtually the constitutional head of the country, the post plays a very vital role during complicated political situations."

Having played a constructive role in politics during the last 30 years, how a "political President" is likely to be different will be evident during his tenure. In recent years, the scope for a "creative presidency" has been circumscribed by well-settled precedents and intense public scrutiny. For instance, no President can ignore the claim of the largest pre-poll coalition to form government. President Kalam, whose presidency was backed by NDA, lost no time in inviting Sonia Gandhi to form government in 2004. In his book, *Turning Point,* he has revealed that there were no reservations about swearing in the Italian-born Congress chief. Similarly, S.D. Sharma invited Atal Bihari Vajpayee to form his 13-day government despite the controversy over the decision. But the present state of political flux can throw up situations that the founding fathers could not have conceived six decades ago. Obviously, the President's job can be as tricky as it is ceremonial.

We now have a president who knows his politics and Constitution and who has demonstrated a rare ability to read the writings on the wall. Finally, presidents come and go after every five years. Each one of them has defined his presidency. If Venkataraman saw his presidency as an "emergency light" which automatically came on in a crisis and went off after it was over, K.R. Narayanan saw himself as 'working president' while APJ Abdul Kalam was the 'people's Prez'. How will Pranab Mukherjee fashion his presidency? The extent to which he will be able to act as a friend, philosopher and guide to the government, and even troubleshoot behind the scenes, will depend on the kind of working relationship he and the prime minister are able to establish in their new roles.

In his acceptance speech on July 25, 2012, he touched upon social and global challenges facing the country. He called for focused action on education, eradication of poverty and fight against corruption to take the country forward. He stressed on the need for a peaceful world, calling it the first ingredient of prosperity. I wish him every success in his endeavours.

Appendix

Excerpts from

President Pranab Mukherjee's Address to the Nation on the eve of 66th Independence Day

It is a great privilege to address, for the first time, my fellow Indians living within our country and in a hundred corners across the globe, on the 65th anniversary of our independence. Words cannot adequately express my gratitude to the people and their representatives for the honour of this high office, even as I am deeply conscious of the fact that the highest honour in our democracy does not lie in any office, but in being a citizen of India, our motherland. We are all equal children before our mother; and India asks each one of us, in whatsoever role we play in the complex drama of nation-building, to do our duty with integrity, commitment and unflinching loyalty to the values enshrined in our Constitution.

It is important to remember, on Independence Day, that in the age of empires freedom was never given; it was taken. It was won by a generation of giants, led by a mighty man of destiny, Mahatma Gandhi, who fought with selfless, unflinching conviction against the mightiest power in history, with a moral force that transformed political thought and whose reverberations echo in great events all around us today. If the rise of European colonisation began in 18th century India, then the rallying cry of "*Jai Hind*!" also signalled its end in 1947. The final call to victory, "Jai Hind!" was given by Subhas Chandra Bose, fondly known to every Indian as "Netaji". Pt. Jawaharlal Nehru, Baba Saheb Ambedkar, Sardar

Vallabhbhai Patel, Maulana Abul Kalam Azad, Sarojini Naidu and many others charted the roadmap of independent India. These extraordinary men and women sacrificed their todays for our tomorrows. That tomorrow has come, and there is a question we must ask ourselves: have we honoured the great vision of these stalwarts, as a nation and as a society?

I was a toddler when Netaji, as Rashtrapati of the 51st Session of Indian National Congress in Haripura, on the banks of the river Tapti, reminded us that "our chief national problems are eradication of poverty, illiteracy and disease". His speech echoed through my home, as it did through millions of others. My father was a freedom fighter and through those long years when freedom seemed an illusion, we were sustained by faith in ourselves, in our leaders, in the strength of non-violence, in the courage of Indians liberated from fear. But we knew then, as we do now, that freedom must mean both bread and dreams.

Netaji and Nehruji believed that India could seize the future by an application of synthesis, samyavada, of what might seem on surface to be implacable opposites. They believed that free India would become, by example, an alternative model for a post-colonial world through economic equity and a social revolution inspired by harmony between communities that had been misled into hostility. Propelled by freedom of faith, gender equality and economic justice for all, India will become a modern nation. Minor blemishes cannot cloak the fact that India is becoming such a modern nation: no faith is in danger in our country, and the continuing commitment to gender equality is one of the great narratives of our times.

❖❖❖

If our economy has achieved critical mass, then it must become a launching pad for the next leap. We need a second freedom struggle; this time to ensure that India is free for ever from hunger, disease and poverty. As my pre-eminent predecessor Dr. Sarvepalli Radhakrishnan, speaking from this platform on the 18th anniversary of freedom, said, "Economic progress is one of the tests of democracy." If progress falls behind rising aspirations, particularly of the young, rage will manifest itself. We are a nation that is becoming younger both in age and spirit; this is an opportunity as well as a challenge. The young thirst for knowledge that will lift their skills; and for opportunity that will put India on the fast track to the first world. They have the character; they need the chance. Education is the seed; and economy is the fruit. Provide good education; disease, hunger and poverty will recede. As I said in my acceptance speech, our motto must be: All for knowledge and knowledge for all. Vision cannot be an open-ended vista; it must be focused on our youth.

❖❖❖

The vigilance on our frontiers has to be matched with vigilance within; we must restore the credibility of those areas of our polity, judiciary, executive and legislature where complacency, exhaustion or malfeasance may have clogged delivery. The people have a right to express their discontent. But we must also understand that legislation cannot be wrenched away from the legislature or justice from the judiciary.

When authority becomes authoritarian, democracy suffers; but when protest becomes endemic, we are flirting with chaos. Democracy is a shared process. We all win or lose together. Democratic temper calls for dignity of behaviour and tolerance of contrary views. Parliament will live by its own calendar and rhythm. Sometimes that rhythm sounds a bit atonal; but in a democracy there is always judgement day, an election. Parliament is the soul of the people, the "*Atman*" of India. We challenge its rights and duties at our peril.

❖❖❖

Old fires that threaten the stability of our nation have not been fully doused; the ash continues to smoulder. It is

particularly painful for me to witness the violence in Assam. Our minorities need solace, understanding and protection from aggression. Violence is not an option; violence is an invitation to greater violence. Concrete attempts have been made to heal the wounds of Assam, including the Assam accord conceived by our young and beloved former Prime Minister Rajiv Gandhi. We should revisit them, and adapt them to present conditions in the spirit of justice and national interest. We need peace for a new economic surge that eliminates the competitive causes of violence.
It is a fact of our geopolitical environment that some problems transcend borders. SAARC was created 27 years ago to find solutions through dialogue, and by mutual cooperation create the rapid economic growth that is the only long-term answer to problems like migration and uneven development. SAARC must acquire vigour to fulfil its mandate.
The SAARC should be a major instrument in the common war against terrorists. Great success is possible by international cooperation. All SAARC nations must cooperate to bring to justice those who believe in mayhem against innocents. There is no other way towards peace on the subcontinent.

I am proud of our brave armed forces and our valiant police forces, who have done so much, at such great personal risk, to curb this menace of terrorism. It is their vigilance which has prevented more havoc. If we sleep in peace it is because they are awake and vigilant in the desolation of desert and mountain and forest; and in the vast loneliness of the seas. I salute their commitment and their patriotism. It is heartening that the armed forces not only guarantee our peace, but also produce medal winners at Olympics. I congratulate all who have done their nation proud at the recently concluded Games, by winning as well as by participating. The number of trophies may not be too large but it is a remarkable improvement upon the last count, Four years later, when I hope to address you again, I am sure, we will celebrate a medals spring.

•